Gravity Cakes!

650+
step-by-step
photos

Gravity Cakes!

Create 45 Amazing Cakes

JAKKI FRIEDMAN & FRANCESCA LIBRAE

Robert
ROSE

Disclaimer

The recipes in this book have been carefully tested by our kitchen and our tasters. To the best of our knowledge, they are safe and nutritious for ordinary use and users. For those people with food or other allergies, or who have special food requirements or health issues, please read the suggested contents of each recipe carefully and determine whether or not they may create a problem for you. All recipes are used at the risk of the consumer.

We cannot be responsible for any hazards, loss or damage that may occur as a result of any recipe use.

For those with special needs, allergies, requirements or health problems, in the event of any doubt, please contact your medical adviser prior to the use of any recipe.

Design and production: Kevin Cockburn/PageWave Graphics Inc.

Editor: Sue Sumeraj

Recipe editor: Jennifer MacKenzie

Proofreader: Kelly Jones

Indexer: Gillian Watts

Photographer: Neil Langan

Cake designs by Jakki Friedman, assisted by Francesca Librae

Cover image: Candy Waterfall (page 55)

Extra images: Dotted backgrounds © iStockphoto.com/ksana-gribakina; Polka dot paper (pages 5, 11 and 35) © iStockphoto.com/billnoll; Baking utensils and ingredients (page 8) © iStockphoto.com/Floortje; Electric mixer (page 12) © iStockphoto.com/Chunhai Cao; Baking bowl (page 13) © iStockphoto.com/karandaev; Sprinkles (page 27) © iStockphoto.com/Jack_Art; Party background (page 46) © iStockphoto.com/kirin_photo; Soda can label (page 102 and 166) © iStockphoto.com/scanrail; Beer can label (page 162) © iStockphoto.com/scanrail.

The publisher gratefully acknowledges the financial support of our publishing program by the Government of Canada through the Canada Book Fund.

Published by Robert Rose Inc.

120 Eglinton Avenue East, Suite 800, Toronto, Ontario, Canada M4P 1E2

Tel: (416) 322-6552 Fax: (416) 322-6936

www.robertrose.ca

Printed and bound in Canada

1 2 3 4 5 6 7 8 9 TCP 25 24 23 22 21 20 19 18 17

CONTENTS

Introduction

From the humble beginner to the master chef, people all over the world are joining an exclusive club of crafty bakers taking on the challenge of gravity baking. Cascading waterfalls of candy falling onto your vanilla cake, or an endless stream of building blocks filling up your chocolate toy box — whichever design you choose, these cakes are sure to impress anyone lucky enough to try them.

You're probably worrying that you need to go out and buy expensive tools and a chainsaw to make these masterpieces come to life. Think again! The only key ingredient you will need to make most of these cakes is an inexpensive balloon stick. All of our gravity cake projects were made in our homes for our kids, friends and loved ones, using tools and ingredients available in most major stores.

Prepare to see facial expressions on your family and friends that you've never seen before. If you start charging a penny for every time you hear "How did you do that?" or "That's amazing!" you'll be rich in no time. It was these very reactions that inspired us to create this book and share our creations with you.

We hope you'll return the favor and share all of your creations with us by posting pictures on our wall at www.facebook.com/Gravitycakes.

PART 1
GETTING STARTED

EQUIPMENT, INGREDIENTS AND TECHNIQUES

Equipment and Tools

There are a seemingly endless number of baking utensils and devices available these days! Many of the tools you will need to make the cakes in this book are already sitting in your kitchen drawer or are easily accessible at an everyday baking supply store or online. As the cake designs increase in difficulty, so will the number of tools you require. Some projects, such as Santa Claus (page 225), require baking pans in a less common size. To make the Rose Garden (page 249), you'll need a piping bag and a specialty decorating tip so you can pipe fluffy icing grass. Make sure to check your project's equipment list before you get going, to ensure that you have everything you need on hand.

In the pages that follow, we've listed the equipment we used to make the projects in this book. Some of the tools are used in nearly every project; others are used in only one or two. Some of these tools are integral to the design of the cake, while others are helpful but not strictly necessary. If you can't locate a circle cutter of the exact size specified, for example, feel free to have a go at cutting circles by hand, or look for another kitchen tool (such as a shot glass) that is approximately the same size to help you stamp out circles. Be creative and have fun!

Think Large with Handheld Mixers

When using a handheld mixer to mix cake batters and icings, make sure to use a large bowl; things can get messy if your bowl isn't big enough.

Electric Mixer

When you're whipping up delicious cakes and butter icing on a regular basis, the ideal tool for the job is a stand mixer. Not only will it free up your hands to get on with other things, but it also ensures an even incorporation of ingredients and comes with various cool attachments for different jobs. But stand mixers aren't for everyone: they can be quite expensive, and they take up quite a bit of room on your countertop, so you may not want to invest in one if you're a casual or occasional cake baker. Not to worry — a handheld electric mixer will also do the trick! They're much more affordable and easier to store.

Cake Pans

Each of the cake projects in this book tells you what size and shape to make your cake layers. Many of the cakes require 8-inch (20 cm) round cake pans that are 2 inches (5 cm) deep, and you could probably get by for quite a while with only that size in your collection. But when you want to expand your horizons into cakes of different sizes, here are the other cake pans used in the projects in this book:

- 4-inch (10 cm) round cake pans (2 inches/5 cm deep)
- 6-inch (15 cm) round cake pans (2 inches/5 cm deep)
- 6-inch (15 cm) square cake pans (2 inches/5 cm deep)
- 7-inch (18 cm) round cake pans (2 inches/5 cm deep)
- 7-inch (18 cm) silicone cupcake mold ($3\frac{1}{2}$ inches/9 cm deep)
- 8-inch (20 cm) square cake pans (2 inches/5 cm deep)
- 10-inch (25 cm) square cake pans (2 inches/5 cm deep)

You will find it useful to purchase at least two pans, because most of the designs call for two to four cake layers. Having multiple pans will save you a lot of time, as the cakes can be baked two at a time.

Either metal or silicone cake pans are fine. If you want to use nonstick pans, that's fine, but make sure they are light in color, as darker pans absorb more heat. (If you must use a dark-colored nonstick pan, reduce the oven temperature by 25°F/10°C.) Line the bottoms of the pans with parchment paper regardless of whether you are using nonstick, then grease the paper and the sides of the pans.

Ovenproof Bowls

A few of the designs in this book require a dome-shaped cake baked in an 8-inch (20 cm) ovenproof bowl. This is the diameter inside the rim at the top of the bowl. Make sure the bowl is around 4 inches (10 cm) deep so it will hold all the batter. Look for a bowl with only a small flat spot on the bottom, as a rounded shape is integral to the design. You can use a metal or silicone bowl, so long as it is ovenproof.

Muffin Pan and Cupcake Liners
If you want to make the Gravity Cupcakes (page 63), you'll need a 12-cup muffin pan and cupcake liners to bake the cupcakes in.

Other Helpful Baking Supplies

Here are some basic cake baking tools you'll want to make sure to have on hand before you get started — you'll find it quite challenging to bake a cake without them!

- **Parchment paper:** Nonstick, greaseproof parchment paper is a very useful item to have on hand when you're making a gravity cake. It can be used to line the bottoms of your cake pans, for easy removal and cleanup, and to wrap around a cake for freezing. We also place some of our molded fondant shapes on parchment paper to let them dry and set before attaching them to the cake.

- **Measuring cups and spoons:** You'll need both a liquid measuring cup (for measuring liquid ingredients) and a set of dry, nesting-style measuring cups (for measuring dry and moist ingredients). Use measuring spoons for amounts under ¼ cup (60 mL). For more information, see "The Science of Baking: Measuring Accurately," page 23.

- **Sifter or fine-mesh sieve:** Sifting the flour before measuring and sifting the dry ingredients into the bowl results in a cake with a much lighter texture than if you just dump the ingredients in from the measuring cup. Plus, sifting helps prevent lumps in ingredients like confectioners' (icing) sugar and unsweetened cocoa powder.

- **Rubber spatula or wooden spoon:** You'll find this tool helpful for scraping as much batter as possible out of the bowl and into the pan, and for smoothing the top of the batter once it's in the pan.

- **Cake tester:** You can purchase a tool dedicated to this purpose or just use a toothpick or skewer instead. Either way, you'll stick the tester into the center of the cake to test for doneness. If the tester comes out clean, the cake is done; if it has batter attached, keep baking.

- **Wire cooling racks:** These are absolutely essential to make sure your cakes cool evenly and don't get soggy bottoms. For our cakes, you'll let them cool in their pans on the racks for 15 minutes, then invert the cakes onto the racks, remove the pans and let the cakes cool completely. It is very, very important that the cakes be fully cooled before you begin assembling and decorating them.

Cake Boards and Other Options

In most of our designs, the cakes are built on top of a 12-inch (30 cm) round cake board. Some cakes, however, use a different size or shape, and others require multiple boards of different sizes and shapes. Cake boards aren't the only option, though — you can build your cake on any type of flat presentation surface, such as a wooden slab or a platter. While we have made suggestions for alternatives in certain projects, we strongly encourage you to be creative and use any presentation surface you like, to add that extra pinch of personality to your design. Why not build your Pancake Stack (page 79) on a large frying pan? Or use a Japanese-inspired serving tray to present your Sushi Selection (page 237)? The possibilities are endless!

Decorating Turntable

As you will be covering most of your cakes in fondant, a decorating turntable will prove to be an invaluable tool. The raised, rotating surface will allow for a smoother distribution of butter icing over the cake and a much easier application of the fondant. You don't have to spend a fortune on this — a standard plastic turntable is fine — just make sure the top is set a few inches from the base and rotates smoothly and easily.

Serrated Knife

Keep a serrated knife handy throughout the decorating process. Most cakes will require leveling (see page 29), and we prefer to use a serrated knife for that task, though a cake leveler will work just fine as an alternative. Some of the more advanced cakes, such as Champagne on Ice (page 193) and Turkey Dinner (page 219), also require some carving to shape the cake (see sidebar, page 29), and a serrated knife will allow you to carve with precision and detail.

We strongly suggest using a large knife, with a blade about 10 inches (25 cm) long. And make sure it's sharp: a blunt knife will prove difficult to maneuver, and you may end up with a misshapen cake!

Palette Knife

A palette knife, also known as an offset spatula, is a wide, flat knife with a rounded tip, and is a must-have in your kitchen arsenal before you begin decorating cakes. Its advantage over a plain old kitchen knife is that it has a flexible blade with a sturdy handle, so it is ideal for spreading icing and perfecting any uneven surfaces with precision and control. The size of the palette knife required will depend on the surface area you are working with. We recommend choosing a larger knife, up to around 14 inches (35 cm) long.

Size Matters

In most cases, the shape of the cake board isn't a requirement, just a recommendation. The size of the board is important, though: if you're switching to a different size than we've called for, make sure the board (or other presentation surface) is at least 2 inches (5 cm) larger than the cake.

Balloon Sticks

Almost all of the cake projects in this book will require you to attach a balloon stick (or two or three) to the center of a cake board using melted candy coating wafers (see page 24). Any standard-size plastic balloon sticks will work well; just make sure they fit the following criteria:

- Choose balloon sticks that are between 15 and 24 inches (38 and 60 cm) in length — the longer the better. You will likely cut them shorter, depending on which cake you're making, but the longer the sticks are to begin with, the more flexibility you will have when deciding how far above the cake you want your display item to hover.
- The balloon sticks must be hollow, because you will be sliding support wires down inside them for added stability and flexibility.
- Make sure the sticks come with cups (the piece at the end of the stick that the balloon would sit on), and that each stick is firmly attached to its cup before you get started. It is the cup that will be submerged in melted candy to affix the stick to the presentation surface. The pieces will never be used separately.

Balloon sticks can be purchased at most party supply stores, but you may find it easier and more economical to purchase them online. In our extensive experience with balloon stick shopping, we have found it much less expensive to purchase bulk quantities of 30 to 60 sticks at a time.

18-Gauge Wires

Sliding support wires down inside your balloon stick adds further stability to your cake and encourages a smoother bend in the stick. We recommend 18-gauge wires because they are strong enough to support your props and thin enough to slide inside the balloon stick. We find that three 18-gauge wires provide the necessary support for just about any gravity cake.

It is possible to structure these cakes without wires; just remember that the more weight on the balloon stick, the more support it will need.

Stick It Good

It is crucial to attach the balloon stick to your presentation surface with melted candy coating wafers, to ensure stability in your cake. You wouldn't want the whole thing to go toppling over just as you're about to wow your guests! Be sure to see page 30 for detailed instructions on attaching the stick, and always let it set until the melted candy has hardened before moving on to the next step of your project.

Cutting the Balloon Stick and Wires to Size

Being able to customize the length of the balloon stick is very helpful because you want your cake, your display item and whatever is falling from the prop to the cake to look proportionate with each other. Each of the projects suggests an appropriate height above the cake that worked well with our props, but since the display items you use may end up being a different size than the ones we found, it's best to use your own judgment when trimming the stick. You may find that your cake looks better with a longer or shorter stick than we suggest.

Wait to trim the stick until you have slid the wires down inside it, so you can cut the stick and wires simultaneously, matching their heights. Cut off just a little bit at a time; you can always cut more off as needed, but once the stick is too short, it's too short!

Kitchen Scale

A reliable kitchen scale is a vital tool for making gravity cakes, as just about every project requires you to weigh out fondant to ensure accuracy in your decorations. A standard-size scale — around 9 by 7 inches (23 by 18 cm) — is fine, and it should be able to determine weights up to at least $2\frac{1}{2}$ lbs (1.25 kg). If the amount of fondant you need for the recipe doesn't fit on the scale all at once, simply divide it in half and weigh half at a time.

Rolling Pin

Rolling out fondant will become a regular pastime once you start creating gravity cakes, so make sure you have a good rolling pin on hand. We recommend purchasing a standard-size rolling pin for larger surface areas and a smaller pin (about 9 inches/23 cm long) for more detailed rolling. We like a wooden pin, but a nonstick rolling pin would also be a great choice for rolling out small pieces of fondant and avoiding any stickiness or tears.

Cake Smoother

After you have covered your cake with a sheet of fondant, you will find a cake smoother essential for smoothing out bumps and wrinkles and creating a perfect finish. You'll get the best use out of a plastic smoother that is roughly 6 by 3 inches (15 by 7.5 cm).

Textured Rolling Pins

Some of the projects call for textured rolling pins to add an extra element of detail to the design. These specialty pins are available at most baking supply stores and online. Remember, most of the time, the textures we suggest are just recommendations; if you have another pattern you prefer, go for it!

Fondant Impression Mats

Fondant impression mats are ideal for adding texture to fondant. Simply press the mat firmly onto the rolled-out fondant and you will see a pretty pattern emerge. Mats are available in several different materials, including plastic and silicone; any material is fine, just look for mats with deep grooves, as shallow ones tend to show up less prominently on the fondant. If you can't find the specific texture we used, pick your favorite alternative!

Ruler

Time to dust off your old stationery ruler! This simple tool will come in very handy when you're making gravity cakes. In addition to helping you measure the dimensions of rolled-out fondant and the lengths of balloon sticks, it will help you cut straight lines when you need fondant strips. Food-safe rulers are available online and in some kitchen stores, but a normal plastic ruler is fine — just make sure you keep it clean and germ-free!

Cutters

You'll want to keep a stash of circle cutters in different sizes on hand for various cakes. If you're looking to create the perfect poker chip, using a circle cutter in the size specified in the project directions will be much easier and more accurate than trying to cut a circle freehand. Circle cutters are sold individually, or you can purchase kits with various sizes included. The cakes in this book use circle cutters in the following sizes:

- $\frac{1}{2}$ inch (1 cm)
- $\frac{5}{8}$ inch (1.5 cm)
- 1 inch (2.5 cm)

- $1\frac{1}{2}$ inches (4 cm)
- 2 inches (5 cm)
- $2\frac{1}{2}$ inches (6 cm)

Alphabet cutters or stamps will also prove useful, allowing you to personalize your design with a loved one's name or a message. Finally, if you plan to make the Wine and Cheese cake (page 243), you'll need a cutter in the shape of a grape leaf.

Cutting Shapes Freehand

If you don't have a cutter in the size or shape you need, just take a stab at cutting freehand using a sharp knife. Alternatively, you can get creative and find a household item, such as an upside-down shot glass, to use as a cutter.

Fondant Molds

Fondant molds are an easy and effective way to create realistic-looking decorations for your cake. Usually made of a bendy rubber or silicone, they can be purchased at most baking supply stores or online. Simply pack the mold with fondant and remove the formed shapes immediately. In some projects, you will use the resulting decorations right away; in others, you will need to let the fondant shapes harden overnight on parchment paper.

Fondant molds are used in the following projects: seashell molds for Beach Party (page 171); building brick molds for Toy Box (page 181); bow molds for Santa Claus (page 225); and button molds for Knitting Basket (page 255). Unless you plan to make one of those designs, you won't *need* to purchase a fondant mold — though they are certainly great tools to have on hand if you want to get creative and add decorations or create designs of your own!

Paintbrushes

You'll want to have some small paintbrushes on hand for painting fondant. Small, delicate areas will require a thin, fine brush; larger surfaces allow for a slightly bigger brush. You will also use a paintbrush to help you attach decorations to your cake and to the balloon stick, dabbing each decoration with water or melted candy coating wafers to use as glue.

You may find it useful to buy a variety pack of small paintbrushes to ensure that you always have the perfect brush on hand.

Pastry Brush

A pastry brush (sometimes called a basting brush or an egg brush) is a large brush that is usually used to glaze pastry with an egg wash. For gravity cakes, you'll be using one to brush large surface areas with water, food coloring, melted candy wafers or a royal icing mixture. When you need to brush liquid over the fondant on a balloon stick, for example, it is much more efficient to use a pastry brush than a fine paintbrush. (For small areas that require precision painting, stick with a paintbrush.)

Silicone pastry brushes tend to reach into small nooks and crannies a little better, while brushes with natural bristles tend to hold on to liquid better, making it easier to spread. Stick with a brush that is 2 inches (5 cm) wide or less; anything larger may make it difficult to brush smaller areas.

Keep 'Em Food-Safe

Stay germ-free by washing your brushes well with soap and water between projects. If you have any concerns about a brush's cleanliness, sterilize it in vodka before using it.

Pastry Bags and Decorating Tips

Since this book's focus is more on fondant decorations than on icing decorations, only a handful of projects require the use of a pastry bag to pipe icing decorations onto the cake. For those projects where you do need a pastry bag (or two), either cloth or disposable pastry bags are absolutely fine. The size of the bag you need will depend on how much icing you are adding to it. Keep medium to large bags on hand to cover all the bases.

As for the decorating tips to attach to the pastry bag, the specific tips used in the designs in this book are:

- A #2 round tip for creating a nest for the Easter Egg Nest (page 107) and piping spaghetti for Spaghetti and Meatballs (page 145).
- A #804 or #2A (1 cm) round tip for icing the Gravity Cupcakes (page 63) and the Giant Cupcake (page 67), and for adding "snow" to the Santa Claus cake (page 225).
- A #233 grass tip for piping grass around the Rose Garden (page 249).

The Wow Factor: An Edible Printer and Frosting Sheets

Only one of the projects in this book (Poker Party, page 167) suggests the use of an edible printer and edible frosting sheets, and even there, we provide alternative ways to create the design by hand. But if you are looking to take your designs to the next level, an edible printer can create incredibly realistic-looking edible decorations. Simply scale an image on your computer to match the dimensions you want and use the edible printer to print the image onto an edible frosting sheet. Using water as glue, attach the sheet to a piece of fondant cut to the same size and shape, attach the decoration to the cake, and you will have the coolest cake in town!

Some very well-stocked baking supply stores may sell this equipment, but you are much more likely to find both edible printers and edible frosting sheets online. Another option, if you don't want to purchase these items but still want their wow factor, is to look online for companies that will print custom edible frosting sheets and ship them to you.

Cake Pop Sticks

Cake pop sticks are normally used to hold — you guessed it — cake pops, but in our projects we use them where needed as support beams, for added stability. (And in the Gravity Cupcakes, page 63, they sub in for balloon sticks.) Depending on the cake, you will need either 6-inch (15 cm) or 3-inch (7.5 cm) cake pop sticks; you can always just purchase the 6-inch (15 cm) sticks and cut them in half when you need 3-inch (7.5 cm) sticks. You'll find cake pop sticks at most supermarkets, at cake shops and online.

Ribbon

Ribbon is wrapped around certain cakes to provide gentle and attractive support. You may need up to 48 inches (100 cm) of ribbon, so make sure you have enough left on your roll. Unless a width is specified, the thickness of the ribbon is entirely up to you; just remember that a wider ribbon may disguise any detail on the sides of your cake.

Food-safe ribbon is available at baking supply stores and online. Alternatively, you can back the ribbon with parchment paper before wrapping it around the cake.

In other cakes, thin ribbon is used to tie props together, as with the chopsticks in Asian Noodles (page 149) or the knitting needles in Knitting Basket (page 255). For these projects, you'll need about 24 inches (60 cm) of ribbon — and make sure it's very thin. In this case, because the ribbon won't be touching the food, there's no need to make sure it's food-safe.

Display Items

For most gravity cakes, you'll need to acquire a miniature prop to use as a display item at the top of the balloon stick. You may be wondering where on earth you're going to find a mini soy sauce bottle for Sushi Selection (page 237) or a mini sand bucket for Beach Party (page 171). For a lot of our cakes, we used mini bottles found at a local supermarket and customized them by adding a fondant handle or printing a label. In other cases, we scoured craft stores, toy stores and thrift stores to find suitable props. You can also order miniature props online, or even raid your child's toy chest! Whenever you're planning to make a gravity cake, think through the design a few days in advance and make sure you can find a suitable item.

Support Dowels

The Ice Cream Birthday Cake (page 187) requires the use of plastic support dowels to stabilize a two-tier cake. These tall, wide, hollow sticks are much larger and sturdier than cake pop sticks, for serious stabilization. They can be purchased at baking supply stores or online.

Change It Up!

If you can't locate the exact prop you see in the photos, think of something else that could take its place. Your creative skills will be put to the test with these cakes, so don't be shy about customizing — especially when it comes to props!

Key Ingredients

Several different components go into building and decorating a gravity cake, so read through your project's ingredient list before you get going, to make sure you have everything you need. Some ingredients are required for every design, while others are needed only for specific projects. If you are struggling to locate an ingredient at your local supermarket, it's always worth checking at a specialty baking supply store or online.

Cakes

Before you can begin crafting a gravity cake, you'll need to bake a cake — or two, or three, or even four! In the next chapter, you will find four delicious cake recipes that you can use to make cakes for any of the projects in this book. But you can also feel free to use your grandma's cake recipe or even use a cake mix from the supermarket to save time (we won't tell anyone, we promise). However you choose to make your cakes, aim for layers that are about $1\frac{1}{2}$ inches (4 cm) high, for the closest resemblance to our cakes and the right proportions for the projects.

The projects tell you how many cakes to make, and what size, but for the most part, they don't specify a flavor. That's because it's really completely up to you! Any flavor will work in any of the projects. In a few, we've suggested a flavor that seems appropriate (for example, chocolate cakes for Gimme S'mores, page 99), but even then you can feel free to change it up.

Cool It!
Make sure to let your cakes cool completely before you begin assembling and decorating them. A cake that isn't completely cooled will melt the icing and is more likely to sink under the weight of fondant.

FREEZING CAKES

In several of the projects, you will need to carve the cake into a custom shape, and this is much easier to do with a frozen cake, which will be less crumbly. To freeze a cake, wrap it in a layer of plastic wrap, then a layer of foil, and freeze for at least 4 hours or up to 2 weeks.

The Science of Baking: Measuring Accurately

When it comes to baking cakes and making icing, measuring your ingredients accurately and consistently is the key to success. For accurate measurements, you'll need three types of measuring tools:

- **A liquid measuring cup:** Liquid ingredients should be measured in a liquid measuring cup, which is typically made of glass or plastic, has a handle and pouring spout, and has graduated markings up the side.
- **Dry, nesting-style measuring cups:** Use these measuring cups for all dry ingredients. They are typically made of stainless steel or plastic and come in sets that include 1 cup (250 mL), ½ cup (125 mL), ⅓ cup (75 mL) and ¼ cup (60 mL) sizes.
- **Measuring spoons:** These typically come in sets of 1 tbsp (15 mL), 1 tsp (5 mL), ½ tsp (2 mL), ¼ tsp (1 mL) and sometimes ⅛ tsp (0.5 mL).

To measure less than ¼ cup (60 mL) of a liquid, pour the liquid into the appropriate measuring spoon (or spoons) just until level with the top edge. To measure ¼ cup (60 mL) or more, place the liquid measuring cup on a level surface and pour in the liquid, bending down to eye level so you can see when the liquid reaches the desired volume as marked on the side of the cup. Scrape out any sticky ingredients, such as honey or oil, from the spoon or cup with a silicone spatula.

To measure less than ¼ cup (60 mL) of a dry ingredient, gently dip the appropriate measuring spoon into the dry ingredient, without packing or tapping, until the spoon is overfilled, then, holding the spoon over the bag or container of the ingredient, place a knife level with the top edge of the spoon and sweep it across the spoon to brush off the excess.

To measure dry ingredients in quantities of ¼ cup (60 mL) or more, use the "spoon-and-sweep" method. Choose the appropriate cup (or cups) and spoon in the dry ingredient until slightly heaping, without packing or tapping the ingredient. Holding the cup over the bag or container of the ingredient, use the edge of a knife to scrape off the excess so the ingredient is level with the top edge of the cup.

The exception to the no-packing rule is brown sugar. Brown sugar should be somewhat firmly packed into the spoon or cup to remove any air that may get trapped between the moist sugar crystals. Properly packed brown sugar should come out of the spoon or cup easily with light tapping, and should hold the shape of the cup or spoon once released.

Butter Icing

While the ingredient list for each project will tell you how much butter icing to make, for most of the cakes you're in charge of choosing the flavor. Use the icing recipes in the next chapter or prepare your own recipe, if you have a favorite. If you have a craving for store-bought icing, that will work too! You'll have your hands full creating beautiful designs, so it's fine to cut corners with a premade butter icing.

TINTING BUTTER ICING

In most of the cakes, the icing ends up covered with fondant, so it doesn't really matter what color it is. However, there are certain cakes that require you to tint some or all of the icing. For those projects, you will need to start with a white icing, such as the Vanilla Butter Icing (page 45), then add gel food coloring, one drop at a time, until you reach the desired color.

Candy Coating Wafers

Almost all of the designs in this book call for candy coating wafers (also known as confectionery coating wafers, molding wafers, coating wafers and Candy Melts). These are small pieces of candy normally sold in bags at well-stocked supermarkets, baking supply stores and craft stores; in some stores, they may also be available in bulk bins. They melt easily and act a lot like melted chocolate, but do not require tempering, as pure chocolate does. They hold extremely firm once dry, acting as an edible glue to add stability to your cake and attach your decorations.

Candy coating wafers are available in a wide range of colors; for these projects, you will likely find white and milk chocolate candy wafers to be the most useful. If a cake requires a specific color, it will be specified in the ingredient list; otherwise, the color is up to you.

Candy coating wafers have a very long shelf life if stored correctly. Store them in an airtight container in a cool, dry place and they will last for up to 18 months. Do not keep them in the refrigerator, as the cold can adversely affect their texture and color.

MELTING CANDY WAFERS

To melt candy coating wafers, place them in a small microwave-safe bowl and microwave on Low (10%) to Medium (50%) power in short blasts — no more than 30 seconds at a time, and less for small amounts. Stir the candy in between blasts, then continue with another blast only if the wafers are not yet fully melted. Melted candy wafers can easily get too hot, and they will get thicker and clumpier the hotter they get. If you overheat candy wafers, discard them and start again; they cannot be saved.

Whitest White

If you're making your own icing, try using colorless vanilla extract instead of the more common brown extract to keep your icing very white in color. This will allow for truer colors when you add the food coloring.

Melted candy coating wafers harden fairly quickly, so for certain tasks that require a little extra time, such as attaching decorations to the balloon stick using melted candy wafers as glue, you may need to remelt the candy. Before you do, add a drop of vegetable oil, mixing it in thoroughly. The oil will loosen up the melted candy and make it less likely to burn while it is reheating.

Fondant

Fondant, also known as fondant icing, is destined to be your constant companion throughout your gravity cake adventures. Fondant is a pliable, dough-like icing that is sweet but mild in flavor, to complement the flavor of your cake. It can be rolled out into a sheet to cover your cake — as is done in most of the projects in this book — and it can be molded into any shape you can imagine, allowing you tremendous flexibility in your designs. It's basically the edible version of modeling clay.

DYING FONDANT

You can purchase colored fondant, but it can be more fun (and is generally cheaper) to just buy white fondant and dye your own, especially if your cake requires multiple colors. Here's how to dye fondant:

1. Prepare a clean work surface, making sure there are no crumbs. If you are worried about staining your surface, place some waxed or parchment paper on top of it.
2. Place a pile of fondant on the surface. Make sure it is nice and soft, as cold fondant can be much harder to knead.
3. Depending on the desired color, add 1 to 3 drops of gel food coloring (or even more, if you're aiming for a deep color). Knead the food coloring into the fondant with the palms of your hands, much like kneading dough.
4. If the color isn't as dark as you'd like, knead in more gel coloring. But be careful not to over-knead the fondant, or it will begin to crack.

KNEADING TWO COLORS TOGETHER

Some of the projects suggest kneading fondant in two colors together to create a particular effect. You might be thoroughly combining two colors to create a whole new shade or just partially combining them to create a streaked, marbled or swirled look that really adds pop and realism to your design. It's very easy to do: just knead the two pieces of fondant together until the desired effect is achieved. Alternatively, you can use a rolling pin to blend the two colors together.

Purchasing Fondant

Depending on how often you plan to use fondant, you may wish to purchase it in bulk. But if you want to buy it on an as-needed basis, check your chosen project to see how much fondant you need; you may find that your supermarket or cake decorating supply store offers a tub in just the right size!

Firming Up Fondant

Certain molded fondant pieces, such as the handle on a beer mug or the loops of a bow, need extra strength to hold their positions. There are two ways to firm these pieces up: you can let them set for 12 to 24 hours, or you can speed up the process by adding CMC (or the brand-name derivative Tylose powder) to the fondant and letting them set for 4 hours. CMC, also known as CMC gum or CMC powder, is the abbreviation for carboxymethyl cellulose — but who wants to remember that? To add CMC to fondant, simply follow the instructions on the CMC package.

STORING FONDANT

When you're creating a gravity cake, you'll be slicing and molding fondant into all sorts of shapes and sizes, so it's inevitable that you'll find yourself with a little left over. To preserve it as long as possible, wrap leftover fondant in plastic wrap or seal it in an airtight container. If using plastic wrap, use several layers to prevent any moisture from reaching the fondant. Store the fondant in a cool, dark area and avoid refrigeration. If stored properly, fondant can be kept for up to 6 months, but for best results, use within 3 to 4 weeks of opening.

Confectioners' (Icing) Sugar

Confectioners' sugar, also known as icing sugar or powdered sugar, is used to whip up delicious butter icing if you're using one of the delicious icing recipes in the book (page 45). We also recommend dusting your work surface with confectioners' sugar before rolling out fondant, to prevent the fondant from sticking. Make sure to have some on hand if you're creating a fondant-heavy design.

Shake Your Sugar Shaker
An easy (and kind of fun) way to dust a work surface with confectioners' (icing) sugar is to place the sugar in a sugar shaker with a fine-mesh top and shake it over the surface.

Confectioners' Glaze

Confectioners' glaze, which is made of food-grade shellac, can be brushed over the entire cake design, or a portion of the design, to create a perfect glossy finish where desired. Remember that the glaze picks up brush strokes and fingerprints, so be careful not to brush over the same area too often — and no touching!

Gel Food Coloring

The projects in this book use the type of soft gel food coloring that comes in squeezable plastic bottles to tint royal icing mixtures, dye fondant and paint texture and details onto fondant. We prefer gel food coloring over liquid food coloring because the color tends to be more concentrated, allowing you to use less. Too much liquid can alter the consistency of fondant, and too much dye may adversely affect the flavor. Gel food coloring is available at some major supermarkets, at baking supply stores and online. If you can only find the type that comes in small pots, use the tip of a paintbrush to scoop out a small amount comparable to a water droplet for each drop of food coloring recommended in the project.

Metallic Edible Paint

Gold and silver edible paints have a unique shimmer and give a more realistic look to certain details, such as the stethoscope for Just What the Doctor Ordered (page 201) or the gold buckles on Chic Handbag (page 259). For larger areas, edible spray paint will save you a lot of time and effort; for smaller details, regular edible paint and a fine paintbrush will work better. Both types of metallic edible paint are readily available at baking supply stores and online.

Royal Icing Mix

Most cake decorators use royal icing mix to create hard icing decorations. In our projects, however, we use it to help us create mixtures with a stiff liquid consistency that resemble other liquids, such as milk in Bowl of Cereal (page 75), tomato soup in Pot of Soup (page 135) or gravy in Turkey Dinner (page 219). It's really easy to whip this mixture up: simply combine the specified amounts of royal icing mix and water, and add food coloring as directed. Remember that you are trying to create a mixture with a stiff liquid consistency — it shouldn't be too runny. Tweak the mixture with more royal icing mix or water as needed.

Sprinkles

For most of the projects that call for sprinkles, feel free to use whatever sprinkles you have on hand or buy an alternative favorite to use in place of the examples in the photographs. For certain designs, though, you'll want to stick pretty close to our recommendation for the sake of realism, such as when using small round white sprinkles to stand in for the sesame seeds on a cheeseburger bun (page 139).

Royal Icing as Glue

Because royal icing mix quickly becomes very hard once it's mixed with water, we also use it as glue in certain designs where extra strength and stability are needed, as with the two-tier Ice Cream Birthday Cake (page 187) or the offset layers on Mother's Day Gift (page 207).

Decorating Techniques

When you first flip through the projects in the book, creating a gravity cake may seem like a daunting task. But once you know all the basic techniques and break each project down into a series of simple steps, creating these gorgeous designs becomes … well, a piece of cake!

Our Lingo

As you make our cakes, you'll notice that we use a lot of the same terms and instructions again and again throughout the methods. But what's the difference between "roll out" and "roll"? Or between "form" and "mold"? Or between "paint" and "brush"? Here's everything you need to know to interpret our lingo.

- **Roll out:** To roll out fondant, you'll need a good strong rolling pin with handles. As with rolling out pastry, the goal is to make the fondant flat and smooth. You'll often be working with an amount large enough to cover your entire cake, so make sure the fondant isn't too cold or hard, or it will be difficult to maneuver. Before you get going, dust your work surface with confectioners' (icing) sugar to prevent the fondant from sticking.

- **Roll:** When instructed to roll fondant into a rounded shape, such as a ball or a tube, all you will need are your two trusty hands. Keep your hands crumb-free and make sure there is confectioners' (icing) sugar on your work surface if you are using it to help you roll the shape.

- **Form:** This means using your hands to form fondant into a specific shape, such as a pacifier for Baby Reveal (page 117) or makeup for Sweet 16 (page 121). Make sure your hands are clean of any crumbs. And don't overhandle the fondant, as this can cause it to crack.

- **Mold:** This instruction means to press fondant firmly over, around or into an object. You'll be molding fondant around a balloon stick in just about every recipe, for example, and in some designs you will mold fondant into a cup or glass. In other cases, you'll want to mold the fondant very snugly over an object so that features of the surface below can be seen through the fondant, as when making the grid in Waffle with Syrup (page 83).

- **Paint:** In our instructions, "paint" means to apply color to a small surface area, such as the dials in Father's Day Barbecue (page 131) or the eye veins in Halloween Cauldron (page 213). When this instruction comes up, a small paintbrush will be your tool of choice.

- **Brush:** Brushing is basically painting, but over a much larger surface area, using either a larger paintbrush or a pastry brush. You might brush melted candy or a royal icing mixture up a balloon stick, or brush food coloring over your cake for a particular effect.

In this section, you'll learn how to level, carve and crumb-coat a cake, how to use balloon sticks for maximum stability and how to cover cakes, cake boards and balloon sticks with fondant. Refer back to these pages often as you start decorating to make sure you stay on the right track.

Once you've learned these basic decorating techniques, you'll be well on your way to joining the exclusive gravity cake club!

Leveling a Cake

Leveling a cake is the process of slicing horizontally across the top to level out the dome shape and create a flat surface. Leveling cakes ensures that they are well balanced and sturdy enough to hold your gravity design.

Make sure your cakes are fully cooled before attempting to level them; otherwise, you'll be cleaning up crumbs!

1. Place the cake, domed side up, on a flat surface.
2. Hold a serrated knife or a cake leveler on one side of the cake, at whatever height is needed to create a level top.
3. Gently slice across the cake, using a sawing motion, until it is completely flat.

Carving a Cake

Some of our projects require customizing the shape of your cake. Don't be daunted by the idea of carving a cake: the instructions in each project will tell you exactly what to do! Just use a large serrated knife and make sure the cake is thoroughly frozen before you begin. It is much easier to carve a frozen cake, as it won't crumble as much. If your freezer is very cold and your cake is too hard to slice through, let it thaw slightly before you carve.

Attaching a Balloon Stick to a Presentation Surface

Before you begin assembling your gravity cake, you need to ensure its stability by firmly attaching your balloon stick (or sticks) to your cake board or other presentation surface. This is a key step that is necessary for most of the projects in the book.

Be Patient
It is very important to wait until the melted candy is fully hardened, securely attaching the balloon stick to the presentation surface, before you move on to the next step in your project.

1. Melt 1 tbsp (15 mL) candy melts as instructed on page 24.
2. Scoop the melted candy into a heap in the center of the presentation surface (or as instructed in a particular project).
3. Make sure the balloon stick is inserted firmly into its cup.
4. Submerge the cup in the melted candy, making sure it is level, and let the candy set for about 20 minutes or until hardened.

Crumb-Coating a Cake

Crumb-coating a cake simply means smearing a layer of icing over it to seal in any crumbs. It's a simple process, but an essential one for the success of the cakes in this book. You'll find it much easier to crumb-coat the cake if you place it on a turntable first.

Most of the projects instruct you to spread a dollop of icing around the base of the balloon stick before sliding the cake down the stick and crumb-coating it. The icing will act as glue between the cake and the presentation surface, further stabilizing the cake.

1. Using a palette knife, gradually spread icing all over the cake, top and sides, until it is completely covered, making sure to hide any grooves in the cake.
2. Move the spatula back and forth until the icing is smooth.
3. Unless otherwise instructed in the project, let the icing set for 30 to 45 minutes (see tip, at right) before moving on to the next step in your project.

Crumb-Coating Tips

• Refrigerating your cake while the icing sets helps the icing retain its moisture, but if you don't have a fridge big enough to fit the cake once it has a balloon stick protruding from it — and who does? — try dabbing the icing lightly with water after it has set.

• You may want to apply a second layer of icing once the first layer has set. This will give your cake a nice smooth finish without any lumps. Each of the projects includes a tip that tells you how much more icing you will need to make should you wish to add this second layer.

Covering a Cake with Fondant

Covering a cake with fondant may seem rather daunting to a newbie cake decorator, but we promise, if you follow our simple instructions, you'll be a pro in no time! Make sure your cake is on a turntable before you begin.

Dust It Up

Dusting your work surface with confectioners' (icing) sugar before rolling out fondant will help prevent the fondant from sticking. Brush off any excess sugar before sliding the fondant onto the cake.

1. Dust a clean work surface with confectioners' (icing) sugar and, using a rolling pin, roll out the amount of fondant specified in your project until it is flat and smooth, making sure it is large enough to cover the entire cake. Use a dry pastry brush to brush off any excess sugar.
2. If your cake's crumb-coating has crusted slightly, dampen the icing with water.
3. Carefully slide the fondant sheet down the balloon stick so it drapes over the cake.
4. Use a cake smoother to gently smooth the top and sides of the cake.
5. Using a sharp knife, trim off any excess fondant around the bottom of the cake, then smooth the cake again.

Covering a Cake Board with Fondant

Some of the projects include a tip with the option of covering the cake board with fondant. In these tips, we suggest a complementary color of fondant to use, and in some cases we also recommend adding texture with a fondant impression mat. But don't be bound by our recommendations — feel free to mix it up and use any color or texture you like!

This process is always done after the cake itself is on the board and has been covered in fondant.

1. Dust a clean work surface with confectioners' (icing) sugar and, using a rolling pin, roll out the specified amount of fondant into a strip about $\frac{1}{8}$ inch (3 mm) thick and long enough to wrap around the entire cake.
2. If you are pressing a texture onto the fondant, do so now.
3. Place the fondant strip on the cake board and carefully wrap it around the cake, covering the cake board completely.
4. Use a cake smoother to create a nice smooth finish.
5. Trim off any excess fondant and smooth over any imperfections.
6. If you applied a texture and it has lost definition during the smoothing process, carefully press the impression mat into the fondant as needed.

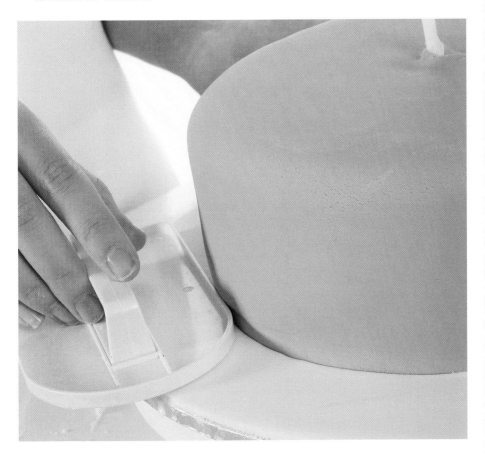

Molding Fondant around a Balloon Stick

Adjust the Width

After molding the fondant around the balloon stick, take a step back to check the results. You may want to remove a pinch of fondant and remold if it appears too thick, or add a pinch more fondant and remold if it looks too thin.

To create the illusion that your display item is floating in midair above your cake, you'll need to cover the balloon stick so that it looks like the contents of the prop are pouring or spilling onto the cake. The first step (and sometimes the only step) in covering the stick is to wrap fondant around it.

1. Roll the amount of fondant specified in your project into a thin tube long enough to cover the portion of balloon stick that will not be hidden by the prop.
2. Press the fondant against the balloon stick and, starting at the top and working down, use your fingers to mold the fondant around the stick.

CAKE AND ICING RECIPES

TIPS

If you don't have superfine sugar, pulse granulated sugar several times in a food processor until it is fine but not powdered, then measure the required volume. Sugar with a fine texture helps produce a fine crumb in your cakes, which makes them sturdy for our projects.

Sifting the flour before measuring and sifting the dry ingredients together helps produce a delicate, fine crumb and is worth the extra effort.

For the best texture in your cakes, beat the butter and sugar together well to incorporate air into your batter. The mixture will become a lighter shade of pale yellow once it has been beaten enough.

Vanilla Cake

- Preheat oven to 350°F (180°C)
- Metal cake pan(s), bottom lined with parchment paper, sides greased and floured

SMALL BATTER

1 cup	sifted all-purpose flour	250 mL
½ tsp	baking powder	2 mL
½ cup	superfine (instant dissolving/berry) sugar	125 mL
6 tbsp	salted butter, softened	90 mL
1	large egg, at room temperature	1
1	large egg yolk, at room temperature	1
¾ tsp	vanilla extract	3 mL
⅓ cup	milk	75 mL

MEDIUM BATTER

1½ cups	sifted all-purpose flour	375 mL
1 tsp	baking powder	5 mL
¾ cup	superfine (instant dissolving/berry) sugar	175 mL
½ cup	salted butter, softened	125 mL
2	large eggs, at room temperature	2
1 tsp	vanilla extract	5 mL
½ cup	milk	125 mL

LARGE BATTER

2 cups	sifted all-purpose flour	500 mL
1½ tsp	baking powder	7 mL
1 cup	superfine (instant dissolving/berry) sugar	250 mL
⅔ cup	salted butter, softened	150 mL
2	large eggs, at room temperature	2
1	large egg yolk, at room temperature	1
1½ tsp	vanilla extract	7 mL
¾ cup	milk	175 mL

EXTRA-LARGE BATTER

2½ cups	sifted all-purpose flour	625 mL
1¾ tsp	baking powder	8 mL
1¼ cups	superfine (instant dissolving/berry) sugar	300 mL

$\frac{3}{4}$ cup + 2 tbsp	salted butter, softened	205 mL
3	large eggs, at room temperature	3
2 tsp	vanilla extract	10 mL
1 cup	milk	250 mL

1. Sift flour and baking powder into a medium bowl. Stir well.
2. In a large bowl, using an electric mixer, beat sugar and butter on medium speed until light and fluffy. Beat in eggs and egg yolk (as called for), one at a time, beating well and scraping the bowl between each addition. Beat in vanilla.
3. Using a silicone spatula, alternately stir in flour mixture and milk, making three additions of flour and two of milk and stirring just until the batter is combined. Spread in prepared pan and smooth the top.
4. Bake in preheated oven until a tester inserted in the center comes out clean. Let cool in pan on a wire rack for 15 minutes, then invert onto the rack, peel off paper and let cool completely.

TO BAKE

- For three 4-inch (10 cm) round cakes, divide the small batter equally among three pans. Bake for 20 to 25 minutes.

- For one 6-inch (15 cm) round or square cake, use the small batter. For two 6-inch (15 cm) square cakes, divide the large batter equally between two pans. Bake for about 30 minutes.

- For two 7-inch (18 cm) round cakes, divide the extra-large batter equally between two pans. Bake for 30 to 35 minutes.

- For one 7-inch (18 cm) silicone cupcake mold, use the large batter. Reduce the oven temperature to 325°F (160°C) and bake for 60 to 65 minutes.

- For one $7\frac{1}{2}$- by $2\frac{1}{2}$-inch (19 by 6 cm) pie plate or baking dish, use the large batter. Reduce the oven temperature to 325°F (160°C) and bake for 50 to 55 minutes.

- For one 8-inch (20 cm) round cake, use the medium batter. Bake for about 30 minutes.

- For one 8-inch (20 cm) square cake, use the large batter. Bake for 30 to 35 minutes.

- For one 8-inch (20 cm) metal bowl, use the large batter. Bake for 60 to 65 minutes. If using an ovenproof glass bowl, reduce the oven temperature to 325°F (160°C) and bake for 55 to 60 minutes.

- For one 10-inch (25 cm) square cake, use a double batch of the large batter. Bake for 35 to 40 minutes.

- For 12 cupcakes, divide the medium batter equally among 12 cups of a paper-lined muffin pan. Bake for about 20 minutes.

TIPS

When dividing batter between two or more pans, use your kitchen scale to help make sure the batter is evenly divided. (First weigh your prepared pans to make sure they are of equal weight, or close to it.)

When you need multiple cake layers for a project, you can double the small, medium or large batters, baking two cakes at a time, but it's best to avoid tripling or more, as it will get more difficult to mix the batter properly and to bake the cakes evenly. The extra-large batter should not be doubled.

When doubling a batter that calls for 1 egg yolk, use 1 whole egg instead.

You want each baked cake layer to be about $1\frac{1}{2}$ inches (4 cm) thick, so trim your cakes as necessary if they are thicker than that (and to level them). Cakes cooked in the silicone cupcake mold should be about $2\frac{1}{2}$ inches (6 cm) thick; cakes cooked in the 8-inch (20 cm) bowl should be about $2\frac{1}{4}$ inches (5.5 cm) thick.

Lemon Cake

- **Preheat oven to 350°F (180°C)**
- **Metal cake pan(s), bottom lined with parchment paper, sides greased and floured**

Lemon zest adds an extra zing of flavor to your gravity cakes. This moist, fluffy cake tastes even better when paired with Lemon Butter Icing (page 45).

TIPS

If you don't have superfine sugar, pulse granulated sugar several times in a food processor until it is fine but not powdered, then measure the required volume. Sugar with a fine texture helps produce a fine crumb in your cakes, which makes them sturdy for our projects.

Sifting the flour before measuring and sifting the dry ingredients together helps produce a delicate, fine crumb and is worth the extra effort.

For the best texture in your cakes, beat the butter and sugar together well to incorporate air into your batter. The mixture will become a lighter shade of pale yellow once it has been beaten enough.

SMALL BATTER

1 cup	sifted all-purpose flour	250 mL
½ tsp	baking powder	2 mL
½ cup	superfine (instant dissolving/berry) sugar	125 mL
6 tbsp	salted butter, softened	90 mL
1	large egg, at room temperature	1
1	large egg yolk, at room temperature	1
2 tsp	grated lemon zest (about 1 lemon)	10 mL
⅓ cup	milk	75 mL

MEDIUM BATTER

1½ cups	sifted all-purpose flour	375 mL
1 tsp	baking powder	5 mL
¾ cup	superfine (instant dissolving/berry) sugar	175 mL
½ cup	salted butter, softened	125 mL
2	large eggs, at room temperature	2
1 tbsp	grated lemon zest (about 2 lemons)	15 mL
½ cup	milk	125 mL

LARGE BATTER

2 cups	sifted all-purpose flour	500 mL
1½ tsp	baking powder	7 mL
1 cup	superfine (instant dissolving/berry) sugar	250 mL
⅔ cup	salted butter, softened	150 mL
2	large eggs, at room temperature	2
1	large egg yolk, at room temperature	1
4 tsp	grated lemon zest (about 2 large lemons)	20 mL
¾ cup	milk	175 mL

EXTRA-LARGE BATTER

2½ cups	sifted all-purpose flour	625 mL
1¾ tsp	baking powder	8 mL
1¼ cups	superfine (instant dissolving/berry) sugar	300 mL

¾ cup + 2 tbsp	salted butter, softened	205 mL
3	large eggs, at room temperature	3
1½ tbsp	grated lemon zest (2 to 3 large lemons)	22 mL
1 cup	milk	250 mL

1. Sift flour and baking powder into a medium bowl. Stir well.

2. In a large bowl, using an electric mixer, beat sugar and butter on medium speed until light and fluffy. Beat in eggs and egg yolk (as called for), one at a time, beating well and scraping the bowl between each addition. Beat in lemon zest.

3. Using a silicone spatula, alternately stir in flour mixture and milk, making three additions of flour and two of milk and stirring just until the batter is combined. Spread in prepared pan and smooth the top.

4. Bake in preheated oven until a tester inserted in the center comes out clean. Let cool in pan on a wire rack for 15 minutes, then invert onto the rack, peel off paper and let cool completely.

TO BAKE

- For three 4-inch (10 cm) round cakes, divide the small batter equally among three pans. Bake for 20 to 25 minutes.

- For one 6-inch (15 cm) round or square cake, use the small batter. For two 6-inch (15 cm) square cakes, divide the large batter equally between two pans. Bake for about 30 minutes.

- For two 7-inch (18 cm) round cakes, divide the extra-large batter equally between two pans. Bake for 30 to 35 minutes.

- For one 7-inch (18 cm) silicone cupcake mold, use the large batter. Reduce the oven temperature to 325°F (160°C) and bake for 60 to 65 minutes.

- For one 7½- by 2½-inch (19 by 6 cm) pie plate or baking dish, use the large batter. Reduce the oven temperature to 325°F (160°C) and bake for 50 to 55 minutes.

- For one 8-inch (20 cm) round cake, use the medium batter. Bake for about 30 minutes.

- For one 8-inch (20 cm) square cake, use the large batter. Bake for 30 to 35 minutes.

- For one 8-inch (20 cm) metal bowl, use the large batter. Bake for 60 to 65 minutes. If using an ovenproof glass bowl, reduce the oven temperature to 325°F (160°C) and bake for 55 to 60 minutes.

- For one 10-inch (25 cm) square cake, use a double batch of the large batter. Bake for 35 to 40 minutes.

- For 12 cupcakes, divide the medium batter equally among 12 cups of a paper-lined muffin pan. Bake for about 20 minutes.

TIPS

When dividing batter between two or more pans, use your kitchen scale to help make sure the batter is evenly divided. (First weigh your prepared pans to make sure they are of equal weight, or close to it.)

When you need multiple cake layers for a project, you can double the small, medium or large batters, baking two cakes at a time, but it's best to avoid tripling or more, as it will get more difficult to mix the batter properly and to bake the cakes evenly. The extra-large batter should not be doubled.

When doubling a batter that calls for 1 egg yolk, use 1 whole egg instead.

You want each baked cake layer to be about 1½ inches (4 cm) thick, so trim your cakes as necessary if they are thicker than that (and to level them). Cakes cooked in the silicone cupcake mold should be about 2½ inches (6 cm) thick; cakes cooked in the 8-inch (20 cm) bowl should be about 2¼ inches (5.5 cm) thick.

Chocolate Cake

This indulgent cake will satisfy all of your chocoholic desires! It's easy, fluffy and delicious — and perfect for decorating.

TIPS

If you don't have superfine sugar, pulse granulated sugar several times in a food processor until it is fine but not powdered, then measure the required volume. Sugar with a fine texture helps produce a fine crumb in your cakes, which makes them sturdy for our projects.

Sifting the flour before measuring and sifting the dry ingredients together helps produce a delicate, fine crumb and is worth the extra effort.

For the best texture in your cakes, beat the butter and sugar together well to incorporate air into your batter. The mixture will become a lighter shade of pale yellow once it has been beaten enough.

- Preheat oven to 350°F (180°C)
- Metal cake pan(s), bottom lined with parchment paper, sides greased and floured

SMALL BATTER

⅔ cup	sifted all-purpose flour	150 mL
⅓ cup	unsweetened cocoa powder	75 mL
¾ tsp	baking powder	3 mL
½ cup	superfine (instant dissolving/berry) sugar	125 mL
6 tbsp	salted butter, softened	90 mL
1	large egg, at room temperature	1
1	large egg yolk, at room temperature	1
⅓ cup	milk	75 mL

MEDIUM BATTER

1 cup	sifted all-purpose flour	250 mL
½ cup	unsweetened cocoa powder	125 mL
1 tsp	baking powder	5 mL
¾ cup	superfine (instant dissolving/berry) sugar	175 mL
½ cup	salted butter, softened	125 mL
2	large eggs, at room temperature	2
½ cup	milk	125 mL

LARGE BATTER

1½ cups	sifted all-purpose flour	375 mL
⅔ cup	unsweetened cocoa powder	150 mL
1½ tsp	baking powder	7 mL
1 cup	superfine (instant dissolving/berry) sugar	250 mL
¾ cup	salted butter, softened	175 mL
2	large eggs, at room temperature	2
1	large egg yolk, at room temperature	1
⅔ cup	milk	150 mL

EXTRA-LARGE BATTER

1¾ cups	sifted all-purpose flour	425 mL
¾ cup	unsweetened cocoa powder	175 mL
1¾ tsp	baking powder	8 mL

1¼ cups	superfine (instant dissolving/berry) sugar	300 mL
¾ cup + 2 tbsp	salted butter, softened	205 mL
3	large eggs, at room temperature	3
1 cup	milk	250 mL

1. Sift flour, cocoa and baking powder into a medium bowl. Stir well and set aside.

2. In a large bowl, using an electric mixer, beat sugar and butter on medium speed until light and fluffy. Beat in eggs and egg yolk (as called for), one at a time, beating well and scraping the bowl between each addition.

3. Using a silicone spatula, alternately stir in flour mixture and milk, making three additions of flour and two of milk and stirring just until the batter is combined. Spread in prepared pan and smooth the top.

4. Bake in preheated oven until a tester inserted in the center comes out clean. Let cool in pan on a wire rack for 15 minutes, then carefully run a knife around the edge of the cake and invert onto the rack. Peel off paper and let cool completely.

TO BAKE

- For three 4-inch (10 cm) round cakes, divide the small batter equally among three pans. Bake for 20 to 25 minutes.

- For one 6-inch (15 cm) round or square cake, use the small batter. For two 6-inch (15 cm) square cakes, divide the large batter equally between two pans. Bake for about 30 minutes.

- For two 7-inch (18 cm) round cakes, divide the extra-large batter equally between two pans. Bake for 30 to 35 minutes.

- For one 7-inch (18 cm) silicone cupcake mold, use the large batter. Reduce the oven temperature to 325°F (160°C) and bake for 60 to 65 minutes.

- For one 7½- by 2½-inch (19 by 6 cm) pie plate or baking dish, use the large batter. Reduce the oven temperature to 325°F (160°C) and bake for 50 to 55 minutes.

- For one 8-inch (20 cm) round cake, use the medium batter. Bake for about 30 minutes.

- For one 8-inch (20 cm) square cake, use the large batter. Bake for 30 to 35 minutes.

- For one 8-inch (20 cm) metal bowl, use the large batter. Bake for 60 to 65 minutes. If using an ovenproof glass bowl, reduce the oven temperature to 325°F (160°C) and bake for 55 to 60 minutes.

- For one 10-inch (25 cm) square cake, use a double batch of the large batter. Bake for 35 to 40 minutes.

- For 12 cupcakes, divide the medium batter equally among 12 cups of a paper-lined muffin pan. Bake for about 20 minutes.

TIPS

When dividing batter between two or more pans, use your kitchen scale to help make sure the batter is evenly divided. (First weigh your prepared pans to make sure they are of equal weight, or close to it.)

When you need multiple cake layers for a project, you can double the small, medium or large batters, baking two cakes at a time, but it's best to avoid tripling or more, as it will get more difficult to mix the batter properly and to bake the cakes evenly. The extra-large batter should not be doubled.

When doubling a batter that calls for 1 egg yolk, use 1 whole egg instead.

You want each baked cake layer to be about 1½ inches (4 cm) thick, so trim your cakes as necessary if they are thicker than that (and to level them). Cakes cooked in the silicone cupcake mold should be about 2½ inches (6 cm) thick; cakes cooked in the 8-inch (20 cm) bowl should be about 2¼ inches (5.5 cm) thick.

You won't believe this scrumptious cake is gluten-free! It's packed with rich chocolate flavor and is a perfect base for your designs.

TIPS

Look for an all-purpose gluten-free flour blend that contains flours and starches, but no added sugar, fat or leavening.

Jakki prefers sunflower oil for baking, but you can use any mild, neutral-tasting oil you prefer.

To make this cake dairy-free, use a plain, unsweetened nondairy milk in place of the milk.

Golden syrup is a thick, sweet syrup popular in Britain. It can be found in jars where British specialty foods are sold and in the baking section of some well-stocked supermarkets. If it's not available, a mild-flavored honey makes a good substitute.

Letting the batter stand before baking allows the gluten-free flours and starches to absorb the liquid, giving the cake a more even surface and crumb inside.

Gluten-Free Chocolate Cake

- Preheat oven to 350°F (180°C)
- Metal cake pan(s), bottom lined with parchment paper, sides greased

SMALL BATTER

¾ cup + 1 tbsp	gluten-free all-purpose flour blend	190 mL
3 tbsp	unsweetened cocoa powder	45 mL
¾ tsp	baking powder	3 mL
⅛ tsp	salt	0.5 mL
3 tbsp	golden syrup or honey	45 mL
½ cup	packed light brown sugar	125 mL
1	large egg, at room temperature	1
⅓ cup	vegetable oil	75 mL
⅓ cup	milk	75 mL

MEDIUM BATTER

1⅓ cups	gluten-free all-purpose flour blend	325 mL
¼ cup	unsweetened cocoa powder	60 mL
1 tsp	baking powder	5 mL
¼ tsp	salt	1 mL
¼ cup	golden syrup or honey	60 mL
1 cup	packed light brown sugar	250 mL
2	large eggs, at room temperature	2
½ cup	vegetable oil	125 mL
½ cup	milk	125 mL

LARGE BATTER

2 cups	gluten-free all-purpose flour blend	500 mL
¼ cup	unsweetened cocoa powder	60 mL
1½ tsp	baking powder	7 mL
½ tsp	salt	2 mL
⅓ cup	golden syrup or honey	75 mL
1⅓ cups	packed light brown sugar	425 mL
3	large eggs, at room temperature	3
⅔ cup	vegetable oil	150 mL
⅔ cup	milk	150 mL

1. Sift flour blend, cocoa, baking powder and salt into a medium bowl. Stir well and set aside.

2. In a small saucepan over low heat, or in a glass measuring cup in the microwave on Medium-Low (30%) power, gently heat the golden syrup until runny. Pour into a large bowl and let cool slightly.

3. Add sugar, egg(s) and oil to the syrup. Using an electric mixer, beat on medium-low speed until well blended and slightly thickened. Beat in milk. Gradually add flour mixture, beating on low speed until batter is smooth. Pour into prepared pan and let stand for 15 minutes.

4. Bake in preheated oven until a tester inserted in the center comes out clean. Let cool in pan on a wire rack for 15 minutes, then carefully run a knife around the edge of the cake and invert onto the rack. Peel off paper and let cool completely.

TO BAKE

- For three 4-inch (10 cm) round cakes, divide the small batter equally among three pans. Bake for 25 to 30 minutes.

- For one 6-inch (15 cm) round or square cake, use the small batter. Bake for about 40 minutes.

- For two 7-inch (18 cm) round cakes, divide the large batter equally between two pans. Bake for about 45 minutes.

- For one 7-inch (18 cm) silicone cupcake mold, use the medium batter. Reduce the oven temperature to 325°F (160°C) and bake for 65 to 70 minutes.

- For one 7½- by 2½-inch (19 by 6 cm) pie plate or baking dish, use the medium batter. Reduce the oven temperature to 325°F (160°C) and bake for 60 to 65 minutes.

- For one 8-inch (20 cm) round cake, use the medium batter. Bake for about 50 minutes.

- For one 8-inch (20 cm) square cake, use the medium batter. Bake for about 45 minutes.

- For one 8-inch (20 cm) metal bowl, use the medium batter. Reduce the oven temperature to 325°F (160°C) and bake for about 85 minutes. If using an ovenproof glass bowl, bake for 65 to 70 minutes.

- For one 10-inch (25 cm) square cake, use a double batch of the medium batter. Bake for about 65 minutes.

- For 12 cupcakes, divide the medium batter equally among 12 cups of a paper-lined muffin pan. Bake for about 25 minutes.

TIPS

When dividing batter between two or more pans, use your kitchen scale to help make sure the batter is evenly divided. (First weigh your prepared pans to make sure they are of equal weight, or close to it.)

When you need multiple cake layers for a project, you can double the small, medium or large batters, baking two cakes at a time, but it's best to avoid tripling or more, as it will get more difficult to mix the batter properly and to bake the cakes evenly.

The height of your baked cake will depend on the gluten-free flour blend you use; some bake up higher than others. You want each baked cake layer to be about 1½ inches (4 cm) thick, so trim your cakes as necessary if they are thicker than that. Cakes cooked in the silicone cupcake mold should be about 2½ inches (6 cm) thick; cakes cooked in the 8-inch (20 cm) bowl should be about 2¼ inches (5.5 cm) thick.

Jumbo Chocolate Chip Cookies

- Preheat oven to 350°F (180°C)
- Two 8-inch (20 cm) round metal cake pans, sides greased, bottoms lined with parchment paper

4 cups	all-purpose flour	1 L
2 tsp	baking powder	10 mL
½ tsp	salt	2 mL
1½ cups	packed light brown sugar	375 mL
½ cup	superfine (instant dissolving/berry) sugar	125 mL
2 cups	salted butter, softened	500 mL
2 tsp	vanilla extract	10 mL
3	large eggs	3
2½ cups	chocolate chips (about 14 oz/400 g)	625 mL

1. In a large bowl, whisk together flour, baking powder and salt. Set aside.
2. In another large bowl, using an electric mixer, beat brown sugar, superfine sugar and butter on medium speed until fluffy. Beat in vanilla, then eggs, until blended.
3. With the mixer on low speed, beat in one-third of the flour mixture until incorporated. Using a wooden spoon, gradually stir in the remaining flour mixture in two additions, stirring until a soft dough forms. Stir in chocolate chips. Divide dough into 6 equal portions, each about 11 oz (330 g).
4. Place 1 portion in a prepared pan. Place a piece of plastic wrap on top and use it to help press the dough neatly into the pan until it is even and fairly smooth. Repeat with another portion and pan. Cover and refrigerate the remaining dough.
5. Bake 2 cookies at a time in preheated oven for 25 to 30 minutes or until golden and tops spring back when lightly pressed in the center. Let cool in pans on wire racks for 5 minutes, then carefully run a knife around the edge of each cookie to loosen. Carefully invert cookies onto racks and peel off paper. Reinvert on the racks, so the tops are facing up, and let cool completely.
6. Let pans cool until just warm. Regrease and line pans, and repeat steps 4 and 5 with the remaining dough. **Makes 6 jumbo cookies.**

Vanilla Butter Icing

²⁄₃ cup	salted butter, softened	150 mL
1 tsp	vanilla extract	5 mL
2½ cups	confectioners' (icing) sugar, sifted	625 mL
2 tbsp	milk	30 mL

1. In a large bowl, using an electric mixer, beat butter on medium speed until very soft, then increase speed to high and beat until smooth and fluffy. Beat in vanilla.
2. With the mixer on low speed, gradually beat in half the sugar, 1 tbsp (15 mL) at a time. Beat in half the milk. Gradually beat in the remaining sugar and milk until incorporated. Gradually increase speed to high and beat until soft and fluffy. **Makes about 2 cups (500 mL).**

Lemon Butter Icing

²⁄₃ cup	salted butter, softened	150 mL
2½ cups	confectioners' (icing) sugar, sifted	625 mL
	Grated zest of 1 lemon	
3 tbsp	freshly squeezed lemon juice	45 mL

1. In a large bowl, using an electric mixer, beat butter on medium speed until very soft, then increase speed to high and beat until smooth and fluffy.
2. With the mixer on low speed, gradually beat in half the sugar, 1 tbsp (15 mL) at a time. Beat in half the lemon zest and lemon juice. Gradually beat in the remaining sugar, lemon zest and lemon juice until incorporated. Gradually increase speed to high and beat until soft and fluffy. **Makes about 2 cups (500 mL).**

Chocolate Butter Icing

2½ cups	confectioners' (icing) sugar, sifted	625 mL
¼ cup	unsweetened cocoa powder	60 mL
²⁄₃ cup	salted butter, softened	150 mL
¼ cup	milk	60 mL

1. Sift sugar and cocoa into a medium bowl. Stir well.
2. In a large bowl, using an electric mixer, beat butter on medium speed until very soft, then increase speed to high and beat until smooth and fluffy.
3. With the mixer on low speed, gradually beat in half the sugar mixture, 1 tbsp (15 mL) at a time. Beat in half the milk. Gradually beat in the remaining sugar mixture and milk until incorporated. Gradually increase speed to high and beat until soft and fluffy. **Makes about 2 cups (500 mL).**

This classic creamy icing is delicious with any cake flavor.

TIP

Butter icing is best used right away, so prepare it just before you're ready to crumb-coat the cakes.

The lemony goodness of this smooth, buttery icing will take your lemon or vanilla gravity cake to zesty new heights!

Smother your cake with an extra layer of chocolate indulgence.

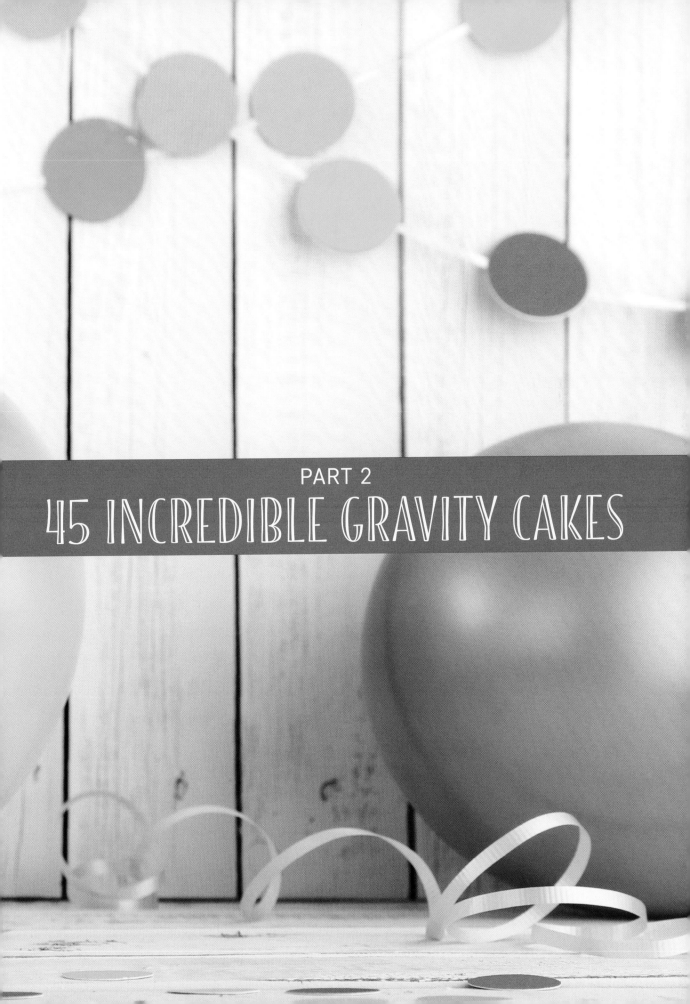

PART 2
45 INCREDIBLE GRAVITY CAKES

EASY CAKES

CHOCOLATE DOME

Here's a beautifully simple design for an aspiring cake decorator and chocolate lover. Just bake your favorite cake in an ovenproof bowl, smother it in icing and decorate it with chocolate candies! Feeds 10.

GETTING STARTED

Melt 1 tbsp (15 mL) candy wafers, attach the balloon stick to the center of the cake board and let set. Spread a small dollop of icing around the base of the stick. Center the cake over the stick and slide it down the stick. Crumb-coat the cake. Slide the 18-gauge wires down inside the stick and trim the stick and wires to the height of the paper bag plus about 5 inches (12.5 cm) from the top of the cake.

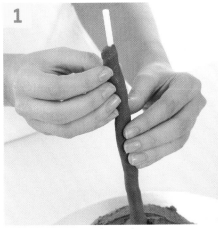

Starting about 1 inch (2.5 cm) below the top and working down, mold the fondant around the balloon stick.

Melt the remaining candy wafers. Using melted candy as glue, and working from the bottom up, cover the entire surface of the cake with candy pieces (see tip, page 52).

EQUIPMENT

- 8-inch (20 cm) ovenproof bowl
- Balloon stick
- 12-inch (30 cm) round cake board
- Three 18-gauge wires
- Small colorful paper bag or small package or box from your chosen candy
- Small paintbrush

INGREDIENTS

- ½ cup (125 mL) candy coating wafers
- 1½ cups (375 mL) chocolate butter icing
- Cake baked in ovenproof bowl (see tip, page 52)
- 1 oz (30 g) brown fondant
- 15 oz (450 g) lightweight candy pieces

Whip up the wow factor with this fun and easy design!

TIPS

Fill the ovenproof bowl only three-quarters full with cake batter, to allow room for expansion.

If you want to add a second layer of icing to the cake before attaching the candy, you will need an additional 1¼ cups (300 mL) icing for this recipe.

When attaching the candy pieces to the cake in step 2 and the balloon stick in step 3, take your time and give each piece time to set before adding another piece above it. If the melted candy starts to harden, add a drop of vegetable oil and reheat.

If using a package or box from your chosen candy, make sure the front is featured when you slide it down the stick.

Using melted candy as glue, attach candy pieces to the fondant on the stick, working from the bottom up and covering as much as will be visible once the paper bag is on the stick.

Using the paintbrush, add a dollop of melted candy to the top of the balloon stick.

Slide the paper bag down the stick (see tip) and hold it in place for about 1 minute, until the candy hardens and secures it.

Attach any remaining candy pieces to the cake board, using melted candy as glue.

Take your
chocolate aspirations
to new heights!

CANDY WATERFALL

Don't be fooled by how masterful this cake looks — it is one of the easiest gravity cakes to make! Feeds 20.

GETTING STARTED

Melt 1 tbsp (15 mL) candy wafers, attach the balloon stick to the center of the cake board and let set. Spread a small dollop of icing around the base of the stick. Center the first cake over the stick and slide it down the stick. Cover the top with icing. Center and slide the second cake down the stick. Crumb-coat the entire cake. Slide the 18-gauge wires down inside the stick and trim the stick and wires to the height of the paper bag plus about 7 inches (18 cm) from the top of the cake.

As soon as possible after crumb-coating the cake, start pressing the double-chocolate wafers to the sides of the cake, standing them on end so they are taller than the cake.

Arrange the wafers side by side all the way around the cake, creating a border around the perimeter at the top of the cake.

Customize this cake with your favorite candy pieces and enjoy the ultimate sweet indulgence.

EQUIPMENT

- Balloon stick
- 12-inch (30 cm) round cake board
- Three 18-gauge wires
- Small colorful paper bag
- 40-inch (100 cm) long colorful ribbon
- Small paintbrush

INGREDIENTS

- ½ cup (125 mL) candy coating wafers
- 2 cups (500 mL) butter icing
- Two 8-inch (20 cm) round cakes, leveled
- 22 double pieces of chocolate-covered wafer biscuit bars (such as KitKat)
- 1 oz (30 g) white fondant
- 15 oz (450 g) lightweight candy pieces (see tip)

TIP

Use a mix of lightweight candy pieces from the bulk bins, in an array of colors and shapes.

TIPS

If you want to add a second layer of icing to the cake before adding the wafers and candies, you will need an additional 1¼ cups (300 mL) icing for this recipe.

When attaching the candy pieces to the balloon stick in step 6, take your time and give each piece time to set before adding another piece above it. If the melted candy starts to harden, add a drop of vegetable oil and reheat.

In step 6, you can cover the fondant all the way up the balloon stick, if you like, but the paper bag will cover much of the top of the stick, so you really only need to conceal the fondant that will not be covered by the bag.

Wrap the ribbon around the cake and tie it in a bow to secure it.

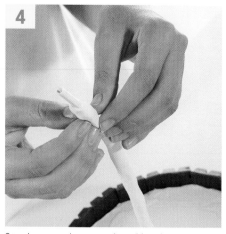

Starting near the top and working down, mold the fondant around the balloon stick. Bend the stick to a natural pouring angle.

Cover the top of the cake with candy pieces until the icing is no longer visible.

Melt the remaining candy wafers and, working with 1 candy piece at a time, use the paintbrush to dab it with melted candy, then attach it to the fondant on the stick (see tips).

Using the paintbrush, add a dollop of melted candy to the top of the balloon stick.

Slide the paper bag down the balloon stick and hold the bag in place for about 1 minute, until the candy hardens and secures it.

DOUBLE CANDY WATERFALL

GETTING STARTED

Melt 2 tbsp (30 mL) candy wafers, attach the balloon sticks about 3 inches (7.5 cm) apart in the center of the cake board and let set. Spread a small dollop of icing around the base of each stick. Center the first cake over the cake board and slide it down the sticks. Cover the top with icing. Center and slide the second cake down the sticks. Crumb-coat the entire cake. Slide three 18-gauge wires down inside each stick and trim the sticks and wires to the height of the paper bags plus about 5 inches (12.5 cm) from the top of the cake.

EQUIPMENT

- 2 balloon sticks
- 12-inch (30 cm) round cake board
- Six 18-gauge wires
- 2 small colorful paper bags or small candy packages or boxes, one for each of your chosen candies
- Small paintbrush

INGREDIENTS

- ¾ cup (175 mL) candy coating wafers
- 2 cups (500 mL) butter icing
- Two 8-inch (20 cm) round cakes, leveled
- 16 double pieces of chocolate-covered wafer biscuit bars (such as KitKat)
- 15 oz (450 g) lightweight candy pieces, in two different varieties
- 2 oz (60 g) white fondant

As soon as possible after crumb-coating the cake, start pressing the double-chocolate wafers to the sides of the cake, standing them on end so they are taller than the cake.

Arrange the wafers side by side most of the way around the cake, creating a border around the perimeter at the top of the cake but leaving a gap at the front.

Easy to make and fun to design with kids!

TIPS

If you want to add a second layer of icing to the cake before adding the wafers and candies, you will need an additional 1¼ cups (300 mL) icing for this recipe.

When attaching the candy pieces to the cake in step 5, cake board in step 6 and balloon stick in step 10, take your time and give each piece time to set before adding another piece above it. If the melted candy starts to harden, add a drop of vegetable oil and reheat.

3

Cover the top of the cake with candy pieces, using the first variety on the left half and the second variety on the right half, until the icing is no longer visible.

4

Starting at the top and working down, mold 1 oz (30 g) fondant around each balloon stick.

5

Melt ¼ cup (60 mL) candy wafers. Using the melted candy as glue, cover the gap at the front of the cake with candy pieces, using the first variety on the left half and the second variety on the right half.

6

Continue the waterfall of candy pieces onto the cake board, using melted candy as glue.

7

Bend the sticks away from each other, creating a natural pouring angle for each stick.

8

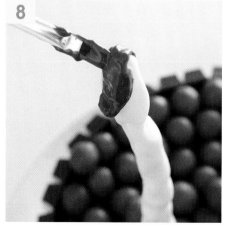

Melt 1 tbsp (15 mL) candy wafers. Using the paintbrush, add a dollop of melted candy to the top of each stick.

9

One at a time, slide each paper bag down a stick (see tip) and hold it in place for about 1 minute, until the candy hardens and secures it.

10

Melt the remaining candy wafers. Using the melted candy as glue, attach candy pieces to the fondant on each stick, using the first variety on the left-hand stick and the second variety on the right-hand stick and covering all the visible fondant.

TIP

If using packages or boxes from your chosen candy, in step 9 make sure to affix each package to the stick on the side of the cake with the matching candy pieces, and make sure the front is featured when you slide it down the stick.

GRAVITY CUPCAKES

These delightful cupcakes are sure to be the star attraction at any celebration. Feeds 12.

GETTING STARTED

Fill the pastry bag with icing and ice each cupcake with a spiral ascending from the edges into the center. Melt 2 tbsp (30 mL) candy wafers (and continue melting more, a little bit at a time, as you use it up in the steps below).

EQUIPMENT

- Pastry bag fitted with a #804 or #2A (1 cm) round tip
- Twelve 6-inch (15 cm) cake pop sticks

INGREDIENTS

- 1½ cups (375 mL) butter icing
- 12 cupcakes in liners (see tip)
- 1 cup (250 mL) milk chocolate candy coating wafers
- 6 mini chocolate bars (see tip, page 64)
- 10 packages of lightweight candy pieces (see tip, page 64)

TIP

It takes the same amount of cake batter to make 12 cupcakes as it does to make an 8-inch (20 cm) cake.

Carefully cut off the end of each chocolate bar package to expose the end of the bar (see tip, page 64). Cut a corner off each candy package.

For each chocolate bar: Dip the top half of a cake pop stick in melted chocolate and slide up through the base of the bar to the middle. Let dry for 1 minute.

Carefully slide the other end of the cake pop stick diagonally into a cupcake, making sure not to press too hard and pierce the bottom.

Spoon melted chocolate around the stick on the cupcake to cover any visible stick and make it appear like the chocolate bar is melting.

TIPS

Avoid chocolate bars that have fillings like wafers; softer chocolate bars will be much easier as you will be sliding your cake pop sticks through the bar.

You will need only 6 candy packages for display, but purchase extras in the same varieties in case you need additional candy pieces for the cupcakes.

When cutting the packages in step 1, ensure that the front of each package will be featured and right side up once it is attached to the cupcake.

When attaching the candy pieces to the sticks in step 8, take your time and give each piece time to set before adding another piece above it. If the melted candy starts to harden, add a drop of vegetable oil and reheat.

5

For the candy packages: Empty all of the candy pieces into piles, dividing them by variety, and set aside.

6

Dip the top of each cake pop stick in melted chocolate. Gently slide a package down each stick and hold it in place for about 1 minute, until the candy hardens and secures it.

7

Carefully slide the other end of each cake pop stick diagonally into a cupcake, making sure not to press too hard and pierce the bottom.

8

Using the melted candy as glue, attach candy pieces to each stick, working from the bottom up (see tip) and matching the candy to the package.

9

Use the remaining candy pieces to decorate the top of each cupcake and hide any visible stick.

These are fun to make and even better to eat!

GIANT CUPCAKE

Simple and classic:
a smaller design
for a more personal
celebration, complete
with an edible
chocolate case —
enjoy! Feeds 12.

GETTING STARTED

Carefully remove the cooled cake from the cupcake mold and cut around the edges of the cake to trim off about ¹/₂ inch (1 cm) from the diameter (see tip, page 68). Clean and dry the mold thoroughly.

EQUIPMENT

- 7-inch (18 cm) silicone cupcake mold (3¹/₂ inches/9 cm deep)
- Balloon stick
- Gold edible spray paint
- 2 pastry bags
- #804 or #2A (1 cm) round tip (see tip, page 68)
- Three 18-gauge wires
- 2 cups (500 mL) cotton balls
- Rubber band

INGREDIENTS

- Cake baked in cupcake mold (see tip, page 68)
- 1²/₃ cups (400 mL) white candy coating wafers
- 1 tbsp (15 mL) candy coating wafers (any color)
- 2¹/₂ cups (625 mL) butter icing, tinted purple
- 1¹/₂ oz (45 g) colored sprinkles

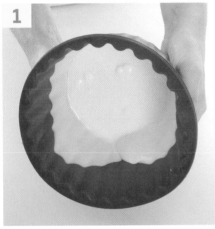

Melt 1 cup (250 mL) white candy wafers and pour into the cupcake mold, rotating it to evenly coat the bottom and sides in candy. Refrigerate for 15 minutes or until the candy is solid. Repeat with another ²/₃ cup (150 mL) white candy wafers.

Gently peel back the mold to release the candy bowl. Trim around the edges of the bowl to create a neat finish, if necessary.

Melt 1 tbsp (15 mL) candy wafers, attach the balloon stick to the center of the candy bowl and let set (see page 30). Spray the outside of the bowl with gold spray and let dry for 25 to 30 minutes.

Coat the inside of the candy bowl with icing. Center the trimmed cake over the balloon stick and slide it down the stick (see tip, page 68).

TIPS

Make sure the hole in the decorating tip is large enough to slide down the balloon stick; if it isn't, choose one that is.

Use the batter from any cake recipe, but fill the silicone cupcake mold only two-thirds full.

You want to trim off about ½ inch (1 cm) from the diameter of the cake to ensure that it will fit inside the candy bowl without any pressure on the cake. If it doesn't quite fit inside the bowl in step 4, trim more off from around the edges until it does.

When sliding the pastry bag down the balloon stick in step 9, make sure the stick slides along the side of the bag, not through the cotton balls.

Fit one of the pastry bags with the round tip and fill with purple icing. Starting from the outer edge of the cake, pipe the icing in a spiral ascending in toward the center.

Use a knife to smooth the icing. Cover the icing with sprinkles.

Slide the 18-gauge wires down inside the balloon stick and trim the stick and wires to the same height. Bend the stick to a natural pouring angle.

Clean the round tip and fit it to the clean pastry bag. Fill the bag with cotton balls. Tie the top of the bag closed with the rubber band.

Slide the pastry bag down the balloon stick (see tip).

Supersize your cupcake and cover with your favorite sprinkles!

GIANT DONUT

GETTING STARTED

Melt the candy wafers, attach the balloon stick to the right side of the cake board, about 3 inches (7.5 cm) from the edge, and let set. Using the circle cutter, cut a hole in the center of the cake. Trim any hard edges from around the cake to create a smoother angle. Spread some icing on the cake board where the cake will sit, to prevent it from sliding. Center the cake above the cake board and slide it down the stick. Crumb-coat the cake. Slide the 18-gauge wires down inside the stick and trim the stick and wires to the height of the sprinkle container plus about 7 inches (18 cm) from the top of the cake.

EQUIPMENT

- Balloon stick
- 12-inch (30 cm) round cake board
- 2½-inch (6 cm) circle cutter
- Three 18-gauge wires
- Clean, empty sprinkle container
- Rolling pin
- Cake smoother
- Pastry brush

INGREDIENTS

- 1 tbsp (15 mL) candy coating wafers
- 8-inch (20 cm) round cake, leveled
- 1¼ cups (300 mL) butter icing
- Confectioners' (icing) sugar
- 20 oz (575 g) cream fondant
- Small bowl of water
- 2⅓ oz (70 g) colored sprinkles
- ½ cup (125 mL) royal icing mix
- Pink gel food coloring

1 Dust your work surface with sugar. Using the rolling pin, roll out 18 oz (525 g) fondant into a sheet large enough to cover the entire cake.

2 Slide the sheet down the balloon stick so it drapes over the cake. Poke and expand a hole in the center of the sheet and use your fingers to mold the fondant into the inner circle. Using the cake smoother, smooth the top and sides of the cake. Trim off any excess fondant.

> Perfect for anyone with an uncontrollable sweet tooth!

TIPS

If you want to add a second layer of icing to the cake before applying the fondant, you will need an additional ⅔ cup (150 mL) icing for this recipe.

In step 4, you can cover the fondant all the way up the stick, if you like, but the sprinkle container will cover some of the top of the stick, so you really only need to conceal the fondant that will not be covered by it.

In step 6, you are trying to create a mixture with a stiff liquid consistency; it shouldn't be too runny. Tweak the mixture with more royal icing mixture or water as needed.

To make the sprinkle container more secure on top of the balloon stick, you can stuff it with cotton balls. If it's a transparent container, brush the inside with melted pink candy coating wafers first.

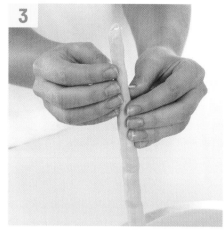

3

Starting at the top and working down, mold the remaining fondant around the balloon stick.

4

Using the pastry brush, brush the fondant on the stick with water. Cover the stick with some of the sprinkles.

5

In a small bowl, combine royal icing mix, 2 tbsp (30 mL) water and 3 drops pink food coloring (or more, as desired).

6

Drizzle over the cake, using the back of a spoon to guide the mixture gently across the surface and over the edges.

7

Sprinkle the pink mixture generously with sprinkles.

8

Slide the sprinkle container down the balloon stick (see tip).

BOWL OF CEREAL

The ideal cake for the serial cereal lover! Choose your loved one's favorite crispy treat to customize an amazing cake that will be the talking point of any party! Feeds 12.

GETTING STARTED

Carefully remove the cooled cake from the cupcake mold and cut around the edges of the cake to trim off about ½ inch (1 cm) from the diameter (see tip, page 76). Clean and dry the mold thoroughly.

1

Melt 1 cup (250 mL) candy wafers and pour into the cupcake mold, rotating it to evenly coat the bottom and sides in candy. Refrigerate for 15 minutes or until the candy is solid. Repeat with another ⅔ cup (150 mL) candy wafers.

2

Gently peel back the mold to release the candy bowl. Trim around the edges of the bowl to create a neat finish, if necessary.

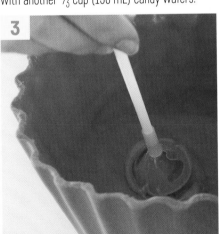

3

Melt 1 tbsp (15 mL) candy wafers, attach the balloon stick to the center of the candy bowl and let set (see page 30).

4

Coat the inside of the candy bowl with icing. Center the trimmed cake over the balloon stick and slide it down the stick (see tips, page 76). Coat the top of the cake with icing.

EQUIPMENT

- 7-inch (18 cm) silicone cupcake mold (3½ inches/ 9 cm deep)
- Balloon stick
- Three 18-gauge wires
- Mini cereal box to match your chosen cereal
- Plastic spoon

INGREDIENTS

- Cake baked in cupcake mold (see tip)
- 1⅔ cups + 4 tbsp (460 mL) candy coating wafers (see tip, page 76)
- 1½ cups (375 mL) butter icing
- 1 oz (30 g) white fondant
- 6 tbsp (90 mL) royal icing mix
- 2 cups (500 mL) cereal

TIP

Use the batter from any cake recipe, but fill the silicone cupcake mold only two-thirds full.

TIPS

You can use any color of candy coating wafers to create the bowl. We love the way this looks with a red bowl. For the stick, use white candy wafers if you're using light-colored cereal, and milk chocolate candy wafers if you're using a darker-colored cereal.

You want to trim off about ½ inch (1 cm) from the diameter of the cake to ensure that it will fit inside the candy bowl without any pressure on the cake. If it doesn't quite fit inside the bowl in step 4, trim more off from around the edges until it does.

If your cake is taller than the candy bowl, trim the top so it sits about ½ inch (1 cm) below the rim of the bowl.

In step 7, the royal icing mixture should have a liquid consistency. Add more water if necessary.

5 Slide the 18-gauge wires down inside the balloon stick and trim the stick and wires to the height of the cereal box plus about 7 inches (18 cm) from the top of the cake. Bend the stick to a natural pouring angle.

6 Working from the top down, mold the fondant around the portion of the stick that will not be covered by the cereal box.

7 In a small bowl, combine royal icing mix and 4 tbsp (60 mL) water (see tip). Pour over the cake, spreading it right to the edges of the bowl.

8 Arrange cereal flakes in the royal icing mixture to look like they are floating in milk. Make sure to leave some of the icing mixture uncovered.

9 Melt 3 tbsp (45 mL) candy wafers and, using the melted candy as glue, attach the remaining cereal flakes to the fondant on the stick.

10 Push the plastic spoon into the cake. Slide the cereal box down the balloon stick, making sure the front is featured.

PANCAKE STACK

Whether you're hiding a chocolate or luscious lemon cake inside this amazing pancake stack, the decadent syrup will add a delicious finish to your design. Feel free to sprinkle on your favorite toppings to customize! Feeds 20.

GETTING STARTED

Melt 1 tbsp (15 mL) candy wafers, attach the balloon stick to the center of the display plate and let set. Spread a small dollop of icing around the base of the stick. Center the first cake over the stick and slide it down the stick. Cover the top with icing. Center and slide the second cake down the stick. Crumb-coat the entire cake. Slide the 18-gauge wires down inside the stick and trim the stick and wires to the height of the syrup bottle plus about 3 inches (7.5 cm) from the top of the cake.

EQUIPMENT

- Balloon stick
- Display plate (minimum 11 inches/28 cm)
- Three 18-gauge wires
- Clean, empty plastic syrup bottle (small to medium)
- Rolling pin
- Pastry brush

INGREDIENTS

- ¾ cup (175 mL) brown candy coating wafers
- 2 cups (500 mL) butter icing
- Two 8-inch (20 cm) round cakes, leveled
- Confectioners' (icing) sugar
- 75 oz (2.1 kg) white fondant
- Brown gel food coloring
- 1 oz (30 g) brown fondant

Dust your work surface with sugar. Divide 55 oz (1.6 kg) white fondant into 12 to 14 equal pieces (see tip, page 80). Using your hands, roll 1 piece into a tube about 20 inches (50 cm) long.

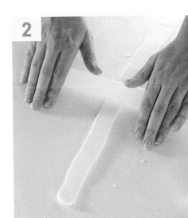

Using the rolling pin, gently roll along the top of the tube to flatten it, making a strip long enough to wrap around the cake.

In a small bowl, combine 3 drops of brown food coloring and ½ cup (125 mL) water (see tip, page 80). Using the pastry brush, lightly brush the top of the strip with food coloring (be careful not to brush the sides).

Wrap the strip, painted side up, around the base of the cake, trim off any excess length and press the ends of the strip together.

TIPS

If you want to add a second layer of icing to the cake before applying the fondant, you will need an additional 1¼ cups (300 mL) icing for this recipe.

The exact number of fondant strips you need to wrap around the cake will depend on how thin you roll them. If you have any extra fondant left from the 55 oz (1.6 kg) used to make strips, add it to the remaining white fondant used in step 6.

Before painting the strips, brush some of the food coloring onto a small scrap of white fondant to test the color for your pancakes. Add more water to dilute the color if necessary.

If your pastry brush isn't giving you the texture you want for your pancake, try blotting the surface lightly with a kitchen towel to encourage a more even blend.

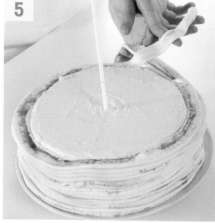

Continue rolling, flattening and painting strips and wrapping them around the cake, placing each one just above the previous one, until you reach the top of the cake.

Roll out the remaining white fondant into a circle large enough to cover the top of the cake with some overhang, trimming it to size as needed. Slide it down the stick to cover the cake.

Using the pastry brush, brush food coloring mixture over the top of the fondant until it resembles a natural pancake texture (see tip). Be careful not to paint the sides.

Working from the top down, mold the brown fondant around the portion of the stick that will not be covered by the syrup bottle, increasing the width of the fondant near the bottom.

Melt the remaining candy wafers and pour the candy in thick lines radiating from the base of the stick to the edges and down the sides of the cake. Guide the candy down the sides with the back of a spoon.

Using the pastry brush, brush candy all over the fondant on the stick. Slide the syrup bottle down the stick.

WAFFLE WITH SYRUP

You'll love this fun cake topped with fresh fruit and melted chocolate — an easy cake for the ambitious beginner, with a few fondant tricks thrown in! Feeds 10.

GETTING STARTED

Melt 1 tbsp (15 mL) candy wafers, attach the balloon stick to the center of the cake board and let set. Spread a small dollop of icing around the base of the stick. Center the cake over the stick and slide it down the stick. Crumb-coat the cake. Slide the 18-gauge wires down inside the stick and trim the stick and wires to the height of the syrup bottle plus about 7 inches (18 cm) from the top of the cake.

EQUIPMENT

- Balloon stick
- 12-inch (30 cm) square cake board
- Three 18-gauge wires
- Mini display syrup bottle
- Rolling pin
- Cake smoother
- Pastry brush

INGREDIENTS

- 1 cup (250 mL) dark brown candy coating wafers
- 1 cup (250 mL) butter icing
- 8-inch (20 cm) square cake, leveled
- 20 oz (575 g) cream fondant
- 2 oz (60 g) dark brown fondant
- 1 cup (250 mL) mixed berries or chopped fruit, washed and thoroughly dried
- Confectioners' (icing) sugar

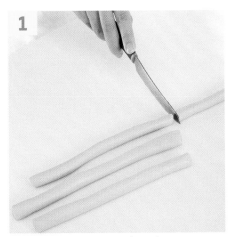

Using your hands, roll 6 oz (175 g) cream fondant into a thin 32-inch (80 cm) tube. Cut the tube into four 8-inch (20 cm) lengths.

Using water as glue, attach the 4 tubes around the top edges of the cake to form a border, trimming off any excess fondant.

Using 1½ oz (45 g) cream fondant, roll 2 tubes the same width as the border and long enough to run across the cake inside the border. Attach the tubes across the cake, dividing it into 3 equal sections.

Using 1½ oz (45 g) cream fondant, roll 6 tubes the same width as the others and long enough to fit crosswise in one of the 3 sections. Attach 2 tubes an equal distance apart in each of the 3 sections, dividing the cake into a grid.

If you want to add a second layer of icing to the cake before applying the fondant, you will need an additional $2/3$ cup (150 mL) icing for this recipe.

To prevent fondant from becoming sticky, dust your work surface with confectioners' (icing) sugar before working with it.

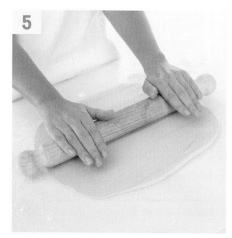

Using the rolling pin, roll out the remaining cream fondant into a sheet large enough to cover the entire cake.

Slide the sheet down the balloon stick so it drapes over the cake. Using your hands, gently mold the fondant over the grid to emphasize the shape.

Use the cake smoother to smooth the sides of the cake. Trim off any excess fondant.

Working from the top down, mold the brown fondant around the portion of the stick that will not be covered by the syrup bottle.

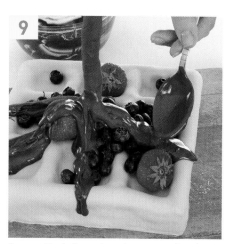

Arrange the fruit on the cake, surrounding the stick, and on the cake board. Melt the remaining candy wafers and drizzle most of it over the fruit on the cake.

Using the pastry brush, paint the fondant on the stick with melted candy. Slide the syrup bottle down the stick. Sprinkle sugar over the entire cake.

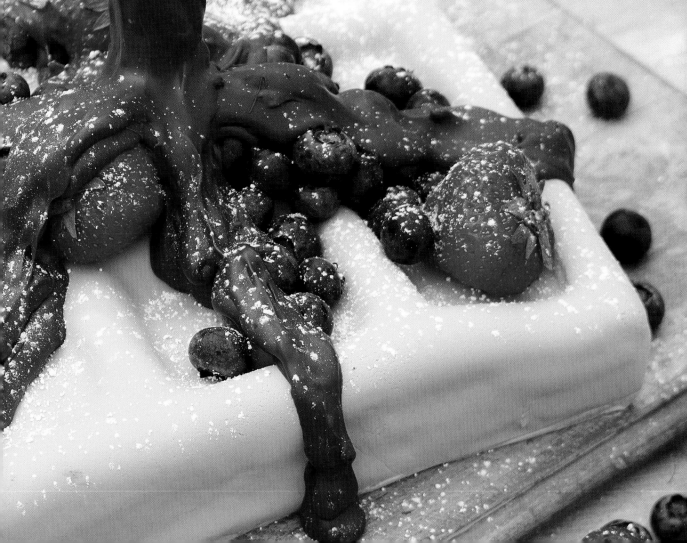

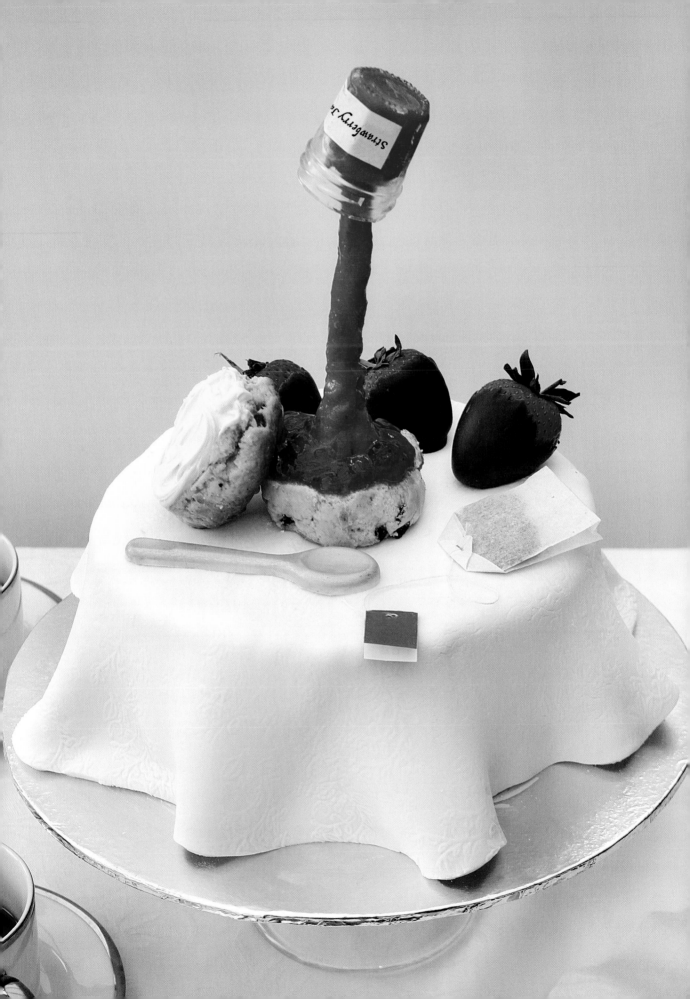

ENGLISH TEA PARTY

Fancy a spot of tea for your more sophisticated guests? This elegant cake will bring a refined charm to any party. Feeds 20.

GETTING STARTED

Melt 1 tbsp (15 mL) white candy wafers, attach the balloon stick to the center of the cake board and let set. Spread a small dollop of icing around the base of the stick. Center the first cake over the cake board and slide the cake down the stick. Cover the top with icing. Center and slide the second cake down the stick. Crumb-coat the entire cake. Slide the 18-gauge wires down inside the stick and trim the stick and wires to the height of the jam jar plus about 3 inches (7.5 cm) from the top of the cake.

EQUIPMENT

- Balloon stick
- 12-inch (30 cm) round cake board
- Three 18-gauge wires
- Clean, empty mini jam jar (jam reserved)
- Rolling pin
- Lace-textured rolling pin
- Pastry brush
- Spoon-shaped candy mold
- Small paintbrush
- Silver edible paint
- Baking sheet, lined with parchment paper

INGREDIENTS

- 5 tbsp (75 mL) white candy coating wafers
- 2 cups (500 mL) butter icing
- Two 8-inch (20 cm) round cakes, leveled
- 24 oz (700 g) white fondant
- 2 tbsp (30 mL) royal icing mix
- Large scone, split in half
- Tea bag with string

continued on next page

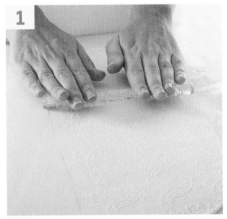

Using the regular rolling pin, roll out the white fondant into a sheet large enough to cover the entire cake. Roll over the sheet with the textured rolling pin.

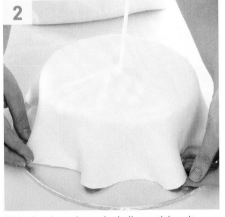

Slide the sheet down the balloon stick so it drapes over the cake, allowing the sides to fall naturally, like the creases of a tablecloth. Trim off any excess fondant.

In a small bowl, combine royal icing mix and 1 tbsp (15 mL) water. Using the pastry brush, brush some of this mixture around the stick in an area as wide as the scone. Slide the bottom half of the scone down the stick.

Using icing mixture as glue, lean the top half of the scone against the bottom half.

INGREDIENTS

- ¼ cup (60 mL) milk chocolate candy coating wafers
- 3 large strawberries
- 1¼ oz (37 g) red fondant
- Jam from mini jar
- 1 tbsp (15 mL) clotted cream

TIPS

If you want to add a second layer of icing to the cake before applying the fondant, you will need an additional 1¼ cups (300 mL) icing for this recipe.

To prevent fondant from becoming sticky, dust your work surface with confectioners' (icing) sugar before working with it.

We suggest making 2 spoons in step 5, just in case one cracks or doesn't form correctly. Run the flat edge of a knife over the mold to scrape off any excess chocolate.

5 Melt the remaining white candy wafers and pour into the spoon mold (see tip). Refrigerate for 10 minutes to harden. Unmold the spoon and, using the small paintbrush, brush it with silver paint. Let dry for 25 to 30 minutes.

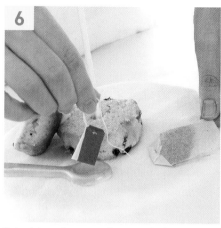

6 Using icing mixture as glue, attach the candy spoon to the top of the cake. Attach the tea bag to the cake.

7 Melt the milk chocolate candy wafers and dip the strawberries in chocolate. Place on the prepared baking sheet and refrigerate for 20 minutes or until the chocolate is hardened.

8 Using the remaining icing mixture as glue, arrange the strawberries on the cake.

9 Stuff ¼ oz (8 g) red fondant into the jam jar and slide the jar down the balloon stick. Working from the top down, mold the remaining red fondant around the stick.

10 Spread jam over the bottom half of the scone. Using the pastry brush, brush jam over the fondant on the stick. Spread clotted cream over the top half of the scone.

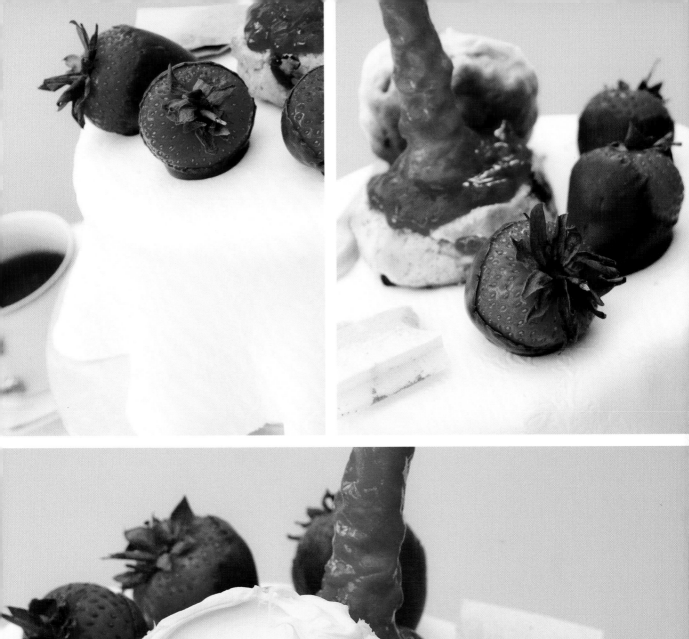

COOKIES AND MILK

For a delicious alternative to a gravity cake, we introduce ... the gravity cookie! Feeds 15.

GETTING STARTED

Melt the candy wafers, attach the balloon stick to the center of the cake board and let see. Trim about 4 inches (10 cm) off the stick. Spread a small dollop of icing around the base of the stick.

Center the first cookie over the stick and slide it down the stick. Smother the top of the cookie with icing so it oozes over the edges. Repeat with the second and third cookies. Center and slide the fourth cookie down the stick.

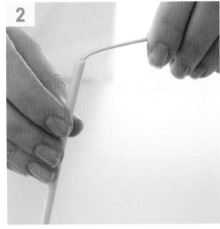

Slide the 18-gauge wires down inside the balloon stick and trim the exposed wires above the stick to a length that will reach halfway inside the plastic cup. Bend the exposed wires to a pouring angle.

> Supersize that classic cookies 'n' milk combo with this four-layer masterpiece oozing with vanilla icing!

EQUIPMENT

- Balloon stick
- 12-inch (30 cm) round cake board
- Three 18-gauge wires
- Lightweight plastic cup
- Thick piece of clear tape
- Rolling pin

INGREDIENTS

- 1 tbsp (15 mL) candy coating wafers
- 2 cups (500 mL) vanilla butter icing (see tip)
- Four 8-inch (20 cm) chocolate chip cookies, cooled (see recipe, page 44, and tips, page 92)
- 7 oz (200 g) white fondant
- Small bowl of water

TIP

Try using colorless vanilla extract to ensure that your icing is extra-white.

TIPS

If desired, bake chocolate candy pieces into the cookie that will top the stack.

While the cookies are still warm, use the balloon stick to stamp a hole through the center of each cookie. This will make it easier to slide them down the stick without breaking them. Enlarge the hole in one cookie a bit and use that one as your base cookie.

If desired, in step 6, after attaching the splotch shape to the cake, pull up the outer edges of the splotch a bit to make it look like the milk is splashing up as it falls.

When attaching the drops and streams to the splotch in step 7, drape the streams over the sides of the cookies so they appear to be milk flowing down.

To prevent fondant from becoming sticky, dust your work surface with confectioners' (icing) sugar before working with it.

3

Working from the top down, mold 2 oz (60 g) white fondant around the balloon stick.

4

Tape the exposed wires to the inside of the plastic cup. Gently mold a small piece of fondant over the tape and wires, blending it down to the fondant on the stick.

5

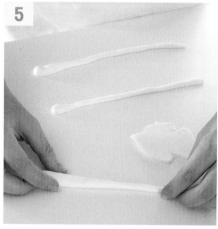

Using the rolling pin, roll out 1 oz (30 g) fondant until thin and smooth. Cut out a loose splotch shape. Use the remaining fondant to create small drops and long, thin streams of milk.

6

Cut a slit halfway down the middle of the splotch shape and place it around the balloon stick on top of the cookie, molding it into place and blending the seam with your fingers (see tip).

7

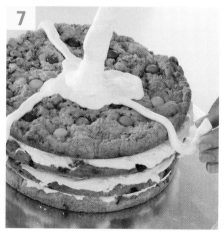

Dampen the splotch with water and attach the streams and some of the drops so that they appear to be flowing from it (see tip), blending any visible seams.

8

Using water as glue, attach a few fondant drops to the cake board.

CHOCOLATE FONDUE

This amazingly gorgeous cake is also amazingly easy! No fondant required — just melted chocolate, icing and fresh strawberries. Feeds 30.

GETTING STARTED

Spread some icing on the cake board where the cake will sit, to prevent it from sliding. Stack the 4 cakes in the center of the cake board, smothering icing between each layer. Crumb-coat the entire cake. Let set for a few minutes, then apply a second coat of icing over the entire cake.

1

Remove the chocolate bar from its package and trim away two-thirds of the package on a diagonal, leaving the bottom third intact. Set the bottom piece aside and discard the top piece.

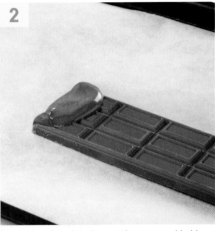

2

Place the chocolate bar on the prepared baking sheet. Melt 5 tbsp (75 mL) candy wafers and spoon some melted chocolate over one end of the chocolate bar.

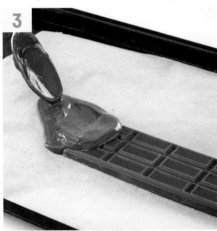

3

Extend the melted chocolate onto the parchment paper in a triangular shape, spooning it in a fairly straight line down from one edge of the chocolate bar and on a diagonal line from the other edge.

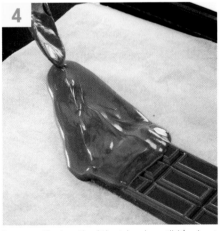

4

Increase the length of the triangle until it's about the same as the height of the cake, making sure the diagonal forms a straight, even line. Refrigerate for 15 minutes or until hardened.

EQUIPMENT

- 12-inch (30 cm) round cake board
- Baking sheet, lined with parchment paper
- 2 fondue sticks

INGREDIENTS

- 7½ cups (1.875 L) vanilla butter icing
- Four 8-inch (20 cm) round cakes, leveled
- Large chocolate bar, still in its package
- 1½ cups (375 mL) milk chocolate candy coating wafers
- 2 large marshmallows
- 10 to 12 strawberries

TIP

In steps 3 and 4, make sure you spoon the chocolate on a diagonal (preferably the same angle used to cut the package), as you will be sliding it into the cake once it has hardened, and you want the chocolate bar to rest at an angle in the cake.

If the melted chocolate starts to harden in steps 6 and 7, add a drop of vegetable oil and reheat.

If you want to secure the strawberries on the cake and cake board, use melted candy wafers as glue.

Peel the hardened chocolate off the parchment paper and set the lined baking sheet aside. Slide the hardened chocolate down into the center of the cake until the attached chocolate bar is resting at an angle on top of the cake.

Melt the remaining candy wafers and spoon chocolate over the top of the cake, using the back of the spoon to guide it down the sides in drips of various lengths.

Skewer the marshmallows with the fondue sticks. Dip the marshmallows and strawberries in chocolate. Place on the lined baking sheet and refrigerate for 20 minutes or until the chocolate is hardened.

Arrange the strawberries on the cake and cake board as desired (see tip). Place the fondue sticks with marshmallows on the cake board. Slide the bottom piece of the package down over the chocolate bar.

This incredible cake will be the talking point of any party!

GIMME S'MORES

GETTING STARTED

Melt 1 tbsp (15 mL) candy wafers, attach the balloon stick to the center of the cake board and let set. Spread a small dollop of icing around the base of the stick. Center the first cake over the cake board and slide the cake down the stick. Cover the top with icing. Center and slide the second cake down the stick. Crumb-coat the entire cake. Slide the 18-gauge wires down inside the stick and trim the stick and wires to the height of the chocolate bar package plus about 7 inches (18 cm) from the top of the cake.

EQUIPMENT

- Balloon stick
- 12-inch (30 cm) round cake board
- Three 18-gauge wires
- Package from your chosen chocolate bar
- 80 inches (200 cm) brown twine
- Small paintbrush
- Cooking torch

INGREDIENTS

- ½ cup (125 mL) milk chocolate candy coating wafers
- 2 cups (500 mL) butter icing
- Two 8-inch (20 cm) round chocolate cakes, leveled
- Eleven 5- by 2½-inch (12.5 by 6 cm) graham crackers (see tip, page 100)
- 2 oz (60 g) brown fondant
- 2 cups (500 mL) large marshmallows
- 13 oz (400 g) chocolate bar pieces

As soon as possible after crumb-coating the cake, press the graham crackers to the sides of the cake, standing them on end so they are taller than the cake and arranging them side by side all the way around.

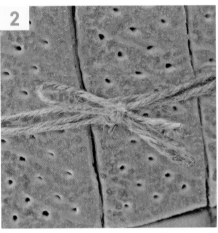

Wrap the twine twice around the cake and tie it in a bow to secure it.

Your guests will drool over this campfire classic in cake form!

TIPS

Purchase rectangular graham crackers that are scored, but not cut.

If you want to add a second layer of icing to the cake before applying the graham crackers and marshmallows, you will need an additional 1¼ cups (300 mL) icing for this recipe.

When attaching the chocolate bar pieces to the balloon stick in step 5, take your time and give each piece time to set before adding another piece above it. If the melted candy starts to harden, add a drop of vegetable oil and reheat.

3

Working from the top down, mold the fondant around the portion of the balloon stick that will not be covered by the candy bar package. Bend the stick to a natural pouring angle.

4

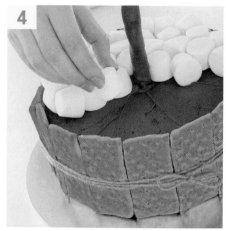

Cover the top of the cake with marshmallows until the icing is no longer visible.

5

Reserve 2 tbsp (30 mL) candy wafers. Melt the remaining candy wafers and, using the melted candy as glue, attach the chocolate bar pieces to the fondant on the stick (see tip).

6

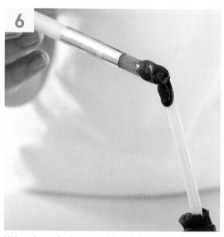

Using the paintbrush, add a dollop of melted chocolate to the top of the balloon stick.

7

Slide the chocolate bar package down the stick and hold the package in place for about 1 minute, until the melted chocolate hardens and secures it.

8

Use the cooking torch across the surface of the marshmallows to create a burnt effect. Melt the reserved candy wafers and drizzle a pool of melted chocolate around the base of the stick.

SODA WITH ICE

Here's a cool cake to celebrate a soda lover on a hot summer day. Feeds 10.

GETTING STARTED

Melt the candy wafers, attach the balloon stick to the center of the cake board and let set. Spread a small dollop of icing around the base of the stick. Center the first cake over the cake board and slide the cake down the stick. Cover the top with icing. Repeat with the second cake. Center and slide the third cake down the stick. Crumb-coat the entire cake. Slide the 18-gauge wires down inside the stick and trim the stick and wires to the height of the soda can plus about 3 inches (7.5 cm) from the top of the cake.

EQUIPMENT

- Balloon stick
- 8-inch (20 cm) round cake board
- Three 18-gauge wires
- Clean, empty soda can
- Rolling pin
- Cake smoother
- Small paintbrush
- Drinking straw

INGREDIENTS

- 1 tbsp (15 mL) candy coating wafers
- 1 cup (250 mL) butter icing
- Three 4-inch (10 cm) cakes, leveled
- Confectioners' (icing) sugar
- 13 oz (400 g) red fondant
- 1½ oz (45 g) white fondant
- 1 oz (30 g) dark brown fondant
- 3 tbsp (45 mL) royal icing mix
- Brown gel food coloring
- 8 clear mints
- 1 tbsp (15 mL) confectioners' glaze
- Lemon slice–shaped candy (optional)

Dust your work surface with sugar. Using the rolling pin, roll out the red fondant into a sheet large enough to cover the entire cake.

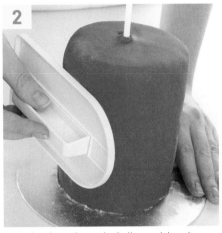

Slide the sheet down the balloon stick so it drapes over the cake. Use the cake smoother to smooth the top and sides of the cake. Trim off any excess fondant. Smooth again.

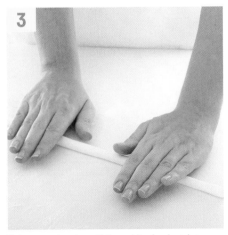

Using your hands, roll the white fondant into a tube long enough to wrap around the cake (about 12.5 inches/31 cm long).

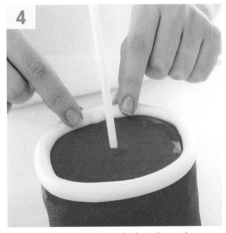

Using water as glue, attach the tube to the top of the cake, around the perimeter. Trim off any excess fondant and press the ends of the tube together.

TIPS

If you want to add a second layer of icing to the cake before applying the fondant, you will need an additional ⅔ cup (150 mL) icing for this recipe.

If desired, after step 4 cover the cake board with 5 oz (150 g) white fondant (see page 33) and press it all the way around with a wood-grain fondant impression mat.

In step 6, you are trying to create a mixture with a stiff liquid consistency; it shouldn't be too runny. Tweak the mixture with more royal icing mixture or water as needed.

Working from the top down, mold the brown fondant around the portion of the balloon stick that will not be covered by the soda can.

In a small bowl, combine royal icing mix and 2 tsp (10 mL) water. Add 4 drops brown food coloring (or as needed for a cola color). Carefully pour most of the mixture over the top of cake, avoiding the white rim.

Using the paintbrush, brush icing mixture up over the fondant on the balloon stick.

Arrange the mints in the icing mixture on the cake, letting them fall naturally in different directions, like ice cubes. Slide the drinking straw into the cake (and bend it if using a bendy straw). Let dry for 1 hour.

Using the cleaned paintbrush, brush the ice cubes and the icing mixture on top of the cake and on the balloon stick with confectioners' glaze.

If desired, place the lemon candy on the cake board. Slide the soda can down the balloon stick.

EASTER EGG NEST

GETTING STARTED

Melt 1 tbsp (15 mL) candy wafers, attach the balloon stick to the center of the cake board and let set. Spread a small dollop of icing around the base of the stick. Center the first cake over the stick and slide it down the stick. Cover the top with icing. Center and slide the second cake down the stick. Crumb-coat the entire cake. Slide the 18-gauge wires down inside the stick and trim the stick and wires to the height of the basket plus about 8 inches (20 cm) from the top of the cake.

Add a thick extra layer of icing around the top border of the cake so it is taller than the rest of the cake.

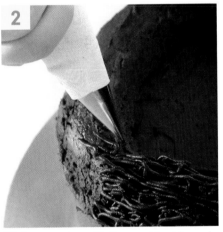

Fill the pastry bag with the remaining icing and pipe long, thin curving lines around the top and edges of the tall icing border, creating the look of a nest.

This cake will help make the holiday extra-special for the kids.

EQUIPMENT

- Balloon stick
- 12-inch (30 cm) round cake board
- Three 18-gauge wires
- Pastry bag fitted with a #2 round tip
- Small wicker basket, stuffed with tissue paper

INGREDIENTS

- ½ cup (125 mL) white candy coating wafers
- 3½ cups (875 mL) chocolate butter icing
- Two 8-inch (20 cm) round cakes, leveled
- 2½ cups (625 mL) mini Easter eggs
- 2 oz (60 g) white fondant

TIP

If you want to add a second layer of icing to the cake, you will need an additional 1¼ cups (300 mL) icing for this recipe.

When attaching the eggs to the balloon stick in step 5, take your time and give each piece time to set before adding another piece above it. If the melted candy starts to harden, add a drop of vegetable oil and reheat.

Cover the top of the cake inside the nest with mini eggs until the icing is no longer visible.

Starting near the top and working down, mold the fondant around the balloon stick. Bend the stick to a natural pouring angle.

Melt the remaining candy wafers. Using the candy as glue, attach mini eggs to the fondant on the stick, covering it almost all the way up (see tip).

Balance the basket on top of the balloon stick.

It's big enough to feed the whole family — and then some!

VALENTINE'S DAY TRUFFLES

A creative alternative to a box of chocolates, this elegant double-layer cake is a sweet way to express your love for a special someone. Feeds 20.

GETTING STARTED

Melt 1 tbsp (15 mL) candy wafers, attach the balloon stick to the center of the cake board and let set. Spread a small dollop of icing around the base of the stick. Center the first cake over the cake board and slide the cake down the stick. Cover the top with icing. Center and slide the second cake down the stick. Crumb-coat the entire cake. Slide the 18-gauge wires down inside the stick and trim the stick and wires to the height of the truffle box plus about 5 inches (12.5 cm) from the top of the cake.

EQUIPMENT

- Balloon stick
- 12-inch (30 cm) round cake board
- Three 18-gauge wires
- Emptied small box of chocolate truffles
- 48 inches (120 cm) ribbon
- Small paintbrush

INGREDIENTS

- ½ cup (125 mL) candy coating wafers
- 2 cups (500 mL) chocolate butter icing
- Two 8-inch (20 cm) round cakes, leveled
- 9 oz (275 g) tall wafer sticks (about 55 sticks)
- 2 oz (60 g) brown fondant
- 9 oz (275 g) individually wrapped chocolates and chocolate truffles (see tip, page 112)
- Red heart-shaped sprinkles

As soon as possible after crumb-coating the cake, start pressing the wafer sticks to the sides of the cake, standing them on end so they are taller than the cake.

Arrange the wafer sticks side by side all the way around the cake, creating a border around the perimeter at the top of the cake.

Show your sweetheart your sweeter side!

TIPS

If you want to add a second layer of icing to the cake before adding the wafers, you will need an additional 1¼ cups (300 mL) icing for this recipe.

Keep some of the chocolates in their wrappers and unwrap others.

When attaching the chocolates to the balloon stick in step 7, take your time and give each piece time to set before adding another piece above it. If the melted candy starts to harden, add a drop of vegetable oil and reheat.

3

Wrap the ribbon around the cake and tie it in a bow to secure it.

4

Starting from the top and working down, mold the fondant around the balloon stick. Bend the stick to a natural pouring angle.

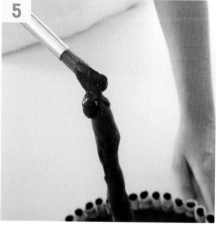

5

Melt the remaining candy wafers and, using the paintbrush, add a dollop of melted candy to the fondant on top of the balloon stick.

6

Slide the truffle box down the balloon stick and hold the box in place for about 1 minute, until the candy hardens and secures it.

7

Working with 1 chocolate at a time, use the paintbrush to dab it with melted candy, then attach it to the fondant on the stick. Cover the stick with chocolates all the way up to the box (see tip).

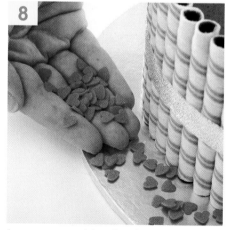

8

Arrange any remaining chocolates on top of the cake. Scatter the heart-shaped sprinkles over the cake and the cake board.

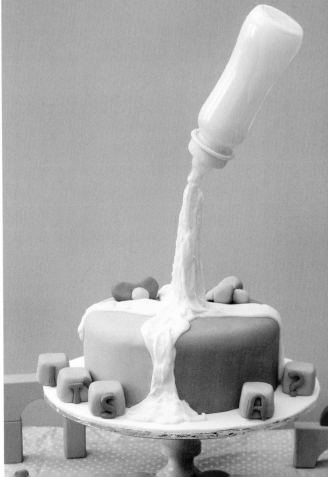

MEDIUM CAKES

BABY REVEAL

Make your big reveal a moment you'll never forget! Feeds 20.

GETTING STARTED

Melt 1 tbsp (15 mL) candy wafers, attach the balloon stick to the center of the cake board and let set. Spread a small dollop of icing around the base of the stick. Center the first cake over the stick and slide it down the stick. Cover the top with icing. Center and slide the second cake down the stick. Crumb-coat the entire cake. Slide the 18-gauge wires down inside the stick and trim the stick and wires to the height of the baby bottle plus about 5 inches (12.5 cm) from the top of the cake.

EQUIPMENT

- Balloon stick
- 12-inch (30 cm) round cake board
- Three 18-gauge wires
- Lightweight baby bottle
- Rolling pin
- Cake smoother
- Pastry brush
- Alphabet cutters (optional)

INGREDIENTS

- 1 cup (250 mL) white candy coating wafers
- 2 cups (500 mL) butter icing
- Two 8-inch (20 cm) round cakes (see tip), leveled
- Confectioners' (icing) sugar
- 16 oz (500 g) pink fondant
- 19 oz (575 g) blue fondant
- 2 oz (60 g) white fondant
- ¼ oz (8 g) cream fondant

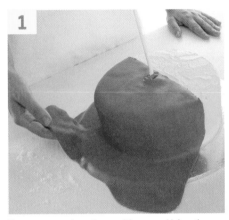

Dust your work surface with sugar. Using the rolling pin, roll out 12 oz (375 g) pink fondant into a sheet big enough to cover half the cake. Slide it down the balloon stick to drape over half the cake.

Roll out 12 oz (375 g) blue fondant and drape over the other half of the cake (no need to slide it down the stick). Smooth the cake and trim off any excess fondant. Smooth again.

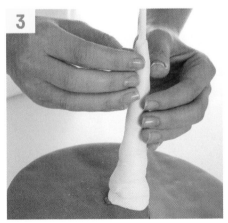

Working from the top down, mold the white fondant around the portion of the balloon stick that will not be covered by the baby bottle, increasing the width of the fondant near the bottom. Bend the stick to a natural pouring angle.

Melt 6 tbsp (90 mL) candy wafers and pour inside the baby bottle. Swirl the melted candy around to coat the inside of the bottle. Screw on the nipple and shake to fill the lid. Set aside to dry (see tip, page 118).

TIP

Before baking your cakes, add blue or pink gel food coloring to the batter to make a colored cake that will reveal your baby's sex when you cut slices.

TIPS

If you want to add a second layer of icing to the cake before applying the fondant, you will need an additional 1¼ cups (300 mL) icing for this recipe.

If desired, after step 2 cover the cake board with 10 oz (300 g) white fondant (see page 33).

The coated bottle will need to set for about 30 minutes after step 4 (or about 15 minutes if you put it in the refrigerator). Make sure it is completely dry before sliding it down the stick in step 10.

To make each pacifier, form most of the blue (or pink) fondant into a half-circle and add an indent to the straight edge with your finger. Roll the remaining blue fondant into a tube and, using water as glue, attach both ends to the half-circle, making a ring. Form the cream fondant into a rounded nipple shape and attach it to the other side of the half-circle.

You will likely need to cut a hole in the bottle's nipple wide enough to slide it down the stick.

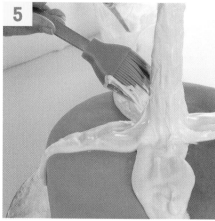

Melt the remaining candy wafers and spoon onto the cake, guiding the candy over the edges with the back of the spoon and completely covering the line between pink and blue. Using the pastry brush, brush candy up the stick.

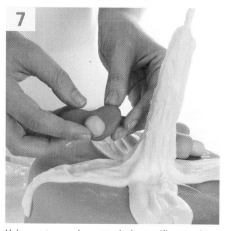

Using water as glue, attach the pacifiers to the top of the cake.

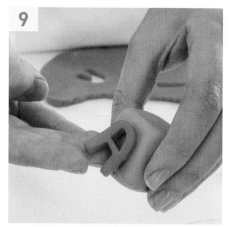

Using the rolling pin, roll out the remaining pink fondant until thin and smooth. Using the alphabet cutters (or a sharp knife), cut out the desired letters. Using water as glue, attach a letter to each block.

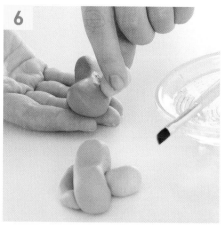

Use 1 oz (30 g) blue fondant and ⅛ oz (4 g) cream fondant to form the shape of a pacifier with ring and nipple (see tip). Repeat step 6 with pink fondant to create another pacifier.

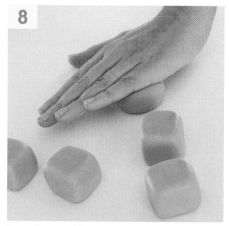

Form the remaining blue fondant into blocks, gently pressing each side against a flat surface.

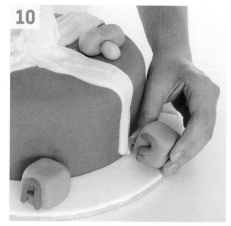

Using water as glue, attach the blocks, letter side forward, in front of the cake on the cake board. Slide the bottle down the balloon stick.

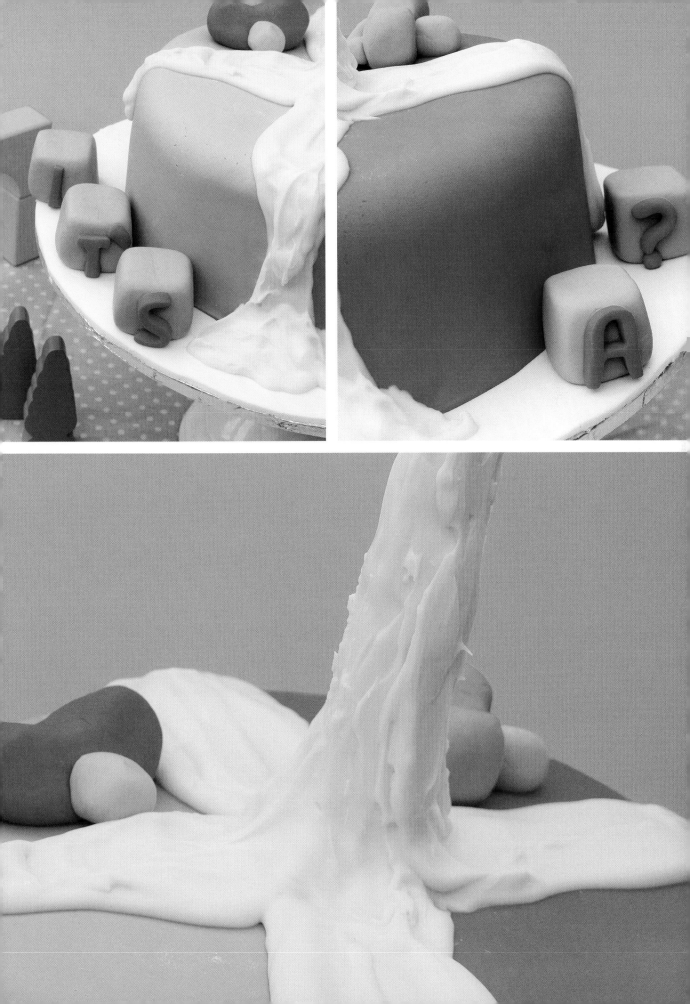

SWEET 16

GETTING STARTED

Melt the candy wafers, attach the balloon sticks about 3 inches (7.5 cm) apart in the center of the cake board and let set. Spread a small dollop of icing around the base of each stick. Center the first cake over the cake board and slide the cake down the sticks. Cover the top with icing. Center and slide the second cake down the sticks. Crumb-coat the entire cake. Slide three 18-gauge wires down inside each stick and trim the sticks and wires to the height of a nail polish bottle plus about 3 inches (7.5 cm) from the top of the cake.

Make a 16th birthday as sweet as can be with this double-layer cake complete with makeup and nail polish in customizable colors! What more could a girl ask? Feeds 20.

EQUIPMENT

- 2 balloon sticks
- 12-inch (30 cm) round cake board
- Six 18-gauge wires
- 2 empty unused nail polish bottles
- Rolling pin
- Cake smoother
- 1½-inch (4 cm) circle cutter
- 1-inch (2.5 cm) circle cutter
- Small paintbrush
- Silver edible paint
- Alphabet cutters (optional)

INGREDIENTS

- 2 tbsp (30 mL) candy coating wafers
- 2 cups (500 mL) butter icing
- Two 8-inch (20 cm) round cakes, leveled
- 24 oz (700 g) bright pink fondant
- 5 oz (150 g) white fondant
- Small bowl of water
- 6 oz (175 g) black fondant

Using the rolling pin, roll out the pink fondant into a sheet large enough to cover the entire cake. Slide the sheet down the balloon stick so it drapes over the cake. Smooth the fondant and trim off any excess. Smooth again.

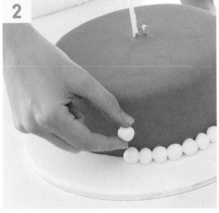

Roll the white fondant into small balls of equal size. Using water as glue, attach the balls all the way around the base of the cake.

Roll 1 oz (30 g) black fondant into a thick, tapered cylinder with a rounded edge at the narrow end. Cut off the wide end to flatten it, forming the handle for a makeup brush.

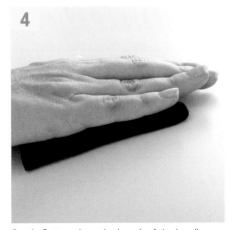

Gently flatten along the length of the handle with the rolling pin or your palm, just enough that it will lie flat.

continued on next page

INGREDIENTS

- ½ oz (15 g) gray fondant
- 1 oz (30 g) brown fondant
- ¼ oz (8 g) blue fondant (see tip)
- ¼ oz (8 g) green fondant
- 3¼ oz (98 g) yellow fondant
- ½ oz (15 g) red fondant
- 3 oz (90 g) purple fondant

TIPS

Use the birthday girl's favorite colors for the makeup and nail polish.

To prevent fondant from becoming sticky, dust your work surface with confectioners' (icing) sugar before working with it.

5

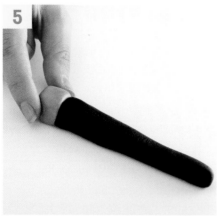

Form ¼ oz (8 g) gray fondant into a block the same size as the flat end of the handle. Using water as glue, attach the block to the handle.

6

Roll the brown fondant into a ball. Using your hand, push down one side of the ball until the shape resembles a makeup brush head. Using water as glue, attach the brush head to the gray block.

7

Using a sharp knife, cut lengthwise lines along the brush head to form bristles, working all the way around and allowing the slices to overlap for a natural effect. Cut crisscross lines into the top of the brush head.

8

For the compacts, use the rolling pin to roll out 2 oz (60 g) black fondant into a thick layer. Cut out 3 circles with the 1½-inch (4 cm) circle cutter.

9

Roll out the blue fondant quite thin and cut out a circle with the 1-inch (2.5 cm) circle cutter. Dampen the top of a black circle and attach the blue circle in the center of the black circle.

10

Repeat step 9 with the green fondant and ¼ oz (8 g) yellow fondant.

11

Roll ½ oz (15 g) black fondant into a thick cylinder, for the lipstick tube. Cut off each end to flatten it.

12

Roll the remaining gray fondant into a short cylinder the same diameter as the black tube. Cut off each end to flatten and shorten it as desired. Using water as glue, attach the cylinder to one end of the tube.

13

Roll the red fondant into a tapered cylinder and cut off the wide end to flatten it. Cut a diagonal flat edge at the narrow end, to resemble a lipstick tip. Attach the lipstick to the gray cylinder.

14

Using the paintbrush, paint the gray fondant on the lipstick and makeup brush with silver paint.

15

Using the tip of the paintbrush or a thin pen, stuff some of the purple fondant inside a nail polish bottle, all the way up to the tip (see tip). Slide the bottle down a balloon stick.

16

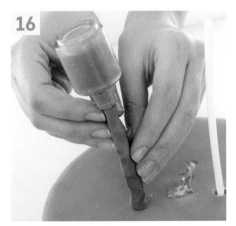

Working from the top down, mold half of the remaining purple fondant around the same stick. Bend the stick outward to a natural pouring angle.

TIPS

If desired, after step 1 cover the cake board with 10 oz (300 g) white fondant (see page 33).

When stuffing the nail polish bottles with fondant in steps 15 and 19, don't overstuff them, as they need to be able to slide down the sticks.

TIP

If you want to add a second layer of icing to the cake before applying the fondant, you will need an additional 1¼ cups (300 mL) icing for this recipe.

17

Roll out the remaining purple fondant until thin and smooth. Cut out a loose splotch shape. Set the excess fondant aside.

18

Cut a slit halfway down the middle of the splotch shape and place it around the purple balloon stick on top of the cake, molding it into place and blending the seam with your fingers.

19

Repeat steps 15 to 17 on the other balloon stick with the remaining yellow fondant.

20

Form the excess purple and yellow fondant into small droplet shapes. Using water as glue, attach them around the splotches on the cake.

21

Roll out the remaining black fondant until thin and smooth. Using the alphabet cutters (or a sharp knife), cut out the desired letters. Using water as glue, attach the letters to the cake and cake board.

22

Using water as glue, arrange the makeup brush, lipstick and compacts on the cake and cake board as desired.

GRADUATION CAP

Hats off to the graduate! Celebrate your loved one with this amazing double-layer cake topped with party poppers! Feeds 15.

GETTING STARTED

Melt the candy wafers, attach the balloon stick to the center of the round cake board and let set. Spread a small dollop of icing around the base of the stick. Center the leveled cake over the stick and slide it down the stick. Cover the top with icing. Center and slide the bowl cake down the stick and carve away any uneven seams where the cakes meet. Crumb-coat the entire cake. Slide the 18-gauge wires down inside the stick and trim the stick and wires to the height of a party popper plus about 7 inches (18 cm) from the top of the cake. Loosely cover the cake with a kitchen towel and set in a cool spot.

EQUIPMENT

- 8-inch (20 cm) round ovenproof bowl
- Balloon stick
- 12-inch (30 cm) round cake board
- Three 18-gauge wires
- Empty party popper
- Rolling pin
- 8-inch (20 cm) thin square cake board
- Cake smoother
- Pastry brush
- Streamers from several party poppers

INGREDIENTS

- 1 tbsp (15 mL) candy coating wafers
- 1½ cups (375 mL) butter icing
- 8-inch (20 cm) round cake, leveled
- Cake baked in ovenproof bowl (see tip, page 128)
- Confectioners' (icing) sugar
- 21 oz (600 g) black fondant
- Small bowl of water
- 1 oz (30 g) white fondant
- 3 oz (90 g) yellow fondant

Dust your work surface with sugar. Using the rolling pin, roll out 5 oz (150 g) black fondant into a sheet large enough to cover the top of the square cake board.

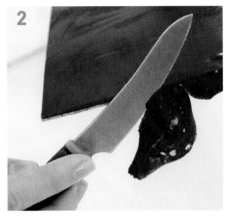

Carefully cut a hole through the center of the square cake board. Dampen the board with water and cover the top with fondant. Smooth the fondant and trim off any excess. Let set for 24 hours (see tip, page 128).

Roll out the remaining black fondant into a sheet large enough to cover the entire cake. Slide the sheet down the balloon stick so it drapes over the cake. Smooth the fondant and trim off any excess.

Align the hole in the square cake board above the balloon stick and slide the board down the stick.

TIPS

Fill the ovenproof bowl only three-quarters full with cake batter, to allow room for expansion.

If you want to add a second layer of icing to the cake before applying the fondant, you will need an additional 1¼ cups (300 mL) icing for this recipe.

Loosely covering the cake with a clean kitchen towel prevents dust from falling on it while you are drying the fondant in step 2. Alternatively, you could prepare the square cake board the day before you start this project.

If you don't have 24 hours to spare for the fondant on the square cake board to set, add CMC (Tylose powder) to the fondant and it will dry in about 4 hours.

There's no method to how you place the streamers — just dangle them until the balloon stick is hidden.

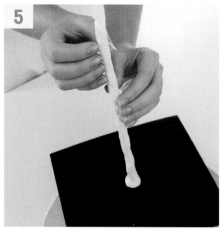

Starting near the top and working down, mold the white fondant around the balloon stick.

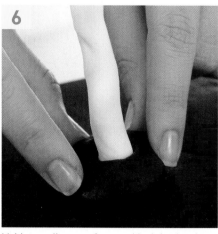

Mold a small scrap of excess black fondant into a circle around the base of the stick.

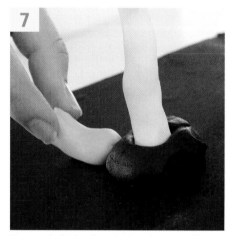

Form a pinch of yellow fondant into a small, thin rectangle about 1 inch (2.5 cm) long. Using water as glue, lay the rectangle flat on the cake and attach one end to the black circle.

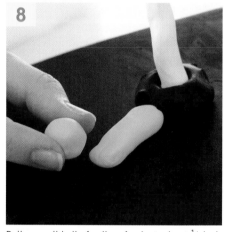

Roll a small ball of yellow fondant, about ½ inch (1 cm) in diameter. Using water as glue, attach the ball to the free end of the rectangle.

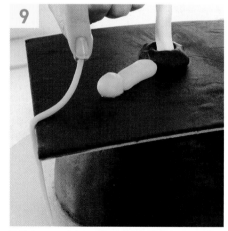

Roll the remaining yellow fondant into several thin strings. Attach each string to the yellow ball and let it trail over the side of the square board. Pinch the seams together where they meet the ball. Trim the strings to desired length.

Using the pastry brush, brush the balloon stick with water. Attach the streamers to the stick, pressing them with your fingers (see tip). Slide the empty party popper down the stick.

FATHER'S DAY BARBECUE

No one can grill quite like Dad, so wow him with this amazing cake instead! Choose his favorite cake to fill this double-layer treat. Feeds 20.

GETTING STARTED

Melt the candy wafers, attach the balloon stick to the center of the cake board and let set. Spread a small dollop of icing around the base of the stick. Center the first cake over the stick and slide it down the stick. Cover the top with icing. Center and slide the second cake down the stick. Crumb-coat the entire cake.

EQUIPMENT

- Balloon stick
- 12-inch (30 cm) round cake board
- Rolling pin
- Cake smoother
- Pastry brush
- Small paintbrush
- Silver edible paint
- Texture fondant impression mat
- Thin, fine paintbrush
- Three 18-gauge wires
- Lightweight silver plastic fork

INGREDIENTS

- 1 tbsp (15 mL) candy coating wafers
- 2 cups (500 mL) butter icing
- Two 8-inch (20 cm) round cakes, leveled
- 25 oz (725 g) red fondant
- 4 oz (125 g) black fondant
- Small bowl of water
- 6½ oz (190 g) gray fondant
- 10 oz (300 g) brown fondant
- Brown gel food coloring
- Black luster dust

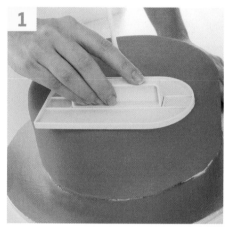

Using the rolling pin, roll out 24 oz (700 g) red fondant into a sheet large enough to cover the entire cake. Slide the sheet down the balloon stick so it drapes over the cake. Smooth the fondant and trim off any excess. Smooth again.

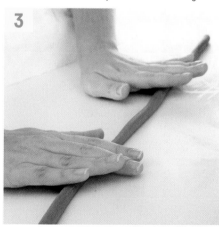

Using your hands, roll 3 oz (90 g) gray fondant into a tube long enough to wrap around the cake (about 25 inches/63 cm long).

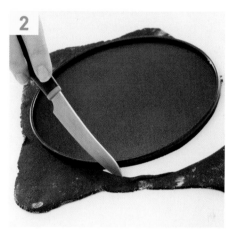

Roll out the black fondant into a 7-inch (18 cm) circle (see tip, page 132). Using the pastry brush, dampen the top of the cake with water. Center the fondant circle over the cake, slide it down the stick and smooth the fondant.

Using water as glue, attach the tube to the top of the cake, around the perimeter. Trim off any excess fondant and press the ends of the tube together.

In step 2, roll out the fondant into a thin sheet, then place a 7-inch (18 cm) pan lid or upside-down bowl on the fondant and use a knife to cut around it.

In step 7, roll the fondant into a ball, then flatten it against a flat surface. Smooth out the rounded edges with the palms of your hands.

To prevent fondant from becoming sticky, dust your work surface with confectioners' (icing) sugar before working with it.

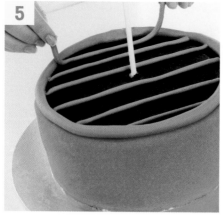

Roll several thin grill bars from the remaining gray fondant, varying their lengths to fit inside the tube on the cake. Dampen the top of the cake and place the bars across the cake, trimming them as needed.

Using the small paintbrush, paint all of the gray fondant with silver paint.

Form 6 oz (175 g) brown fondant into 2 burger patties (see tip). Press the patties with the impression mat and smooth with your finger. Use the blunt edge of a knife to make 3 indents across each burger.

In a small bowl, combine 1 drop brown food coloring and 2 tsp (10 mL) water. Using the pastry brush, brush the food coloring over the tops of the burger patties.

Using the thin paintbrush, dab black luster dust into the indents on the patties to create a charcoal burn effect.

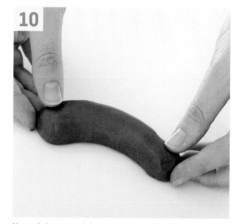

Knead the remaining red fondant into the remaining brown fondant until you reach the desired reddish color. Divide the fondant in half and form into 2 loose sausage shapes.

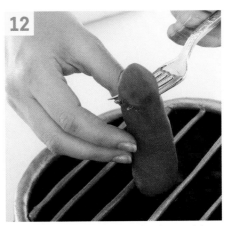

11

Slide the 18-gauge wires down inside the balloon stick and trim the stick and wires to slightly less than the height of a sausage standing on end. Bend the stick to a slight angle. Slide a sausage down the stick.

12

Mold the sausage into a slight bend around the stick. Push the tines of the fork through the top of the sausage so the fork is held firmly in place.

13

Using water as glue, attach the burger patties to the grill. Shape the remaining sausage as desired and attach it to the grill.

14

Use the blunt edge of a knife to make indents across both sausages. Brush the sausages with food coloring, then dab the indents with luster dust.

15

Form the remaining gray fondant into 3 disks and 3 rectangles that will fit across the disks. Using water as glue, attach a rectangle to each disk, to form dials.

16

Dampen the front of the cake and attach the dials to the cake, with the rectangles pointing in different directions. Paint the dials with silver paint.

TIPS

If you want to add a second layer of icing to the cake before applying the fondant, you will need an additional 1¼ cups (300 mL) icing for this recipe.

If desired, after step 1 cover the cake board with 10 oz (300 g) black fondant (see page 33).

POT OF SOUP

Here's a nice hearty cake for a cozy winter dinner party. Feeds 25.

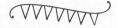

GETTING STARTED

Melt the candy wafers, attach the balloon stick to the center of the cake board and let set. Spread a small dollop of icing around the base of the stick. Center the first cake over the stick and slide it down the stick. Cover the top with icing. Repeat with the second cake. Center and slide the third cake down the stick. Crumb-coat the entire cake and let set for 15 minutes. Slide the 18-gauge wires down inside the stick and trim the stick and wires to the height of the soup can plus about 7 inches (18 cm) from the top of the cake.

EQUIPMENT

- Balloon stick
- 12-inch (30 cm) round cake board
- Three 18-gauge wires
- Clean, empty soup can
- Rolling pin
- Cake smoother
- Parchment paper
- Two 3-inch (7.5 cm) cake pop sticks, each cut in half
- Pastry brush
- Large spoon (optional)

INGREDIENTS

- 1 tbsp (15 mL) candy coating wafers
- 2½ cups (625 mL) butter icing
- Three 8-inch (20 cm) round cakes, leveled
- 37 oz (1.1 kg) gray fondant
- Small bowl of water
- Silver edible spray paint
- 1 oz (30 g) orange fondant
- ¼ oz (8 g) green fondant
- ¼ oz (8 g) yellow fondant
- Red gel food coloring
- Yellow gel food coloring
- Orange gel food coloring
- ¾ cup (175 mL) royal icing mix

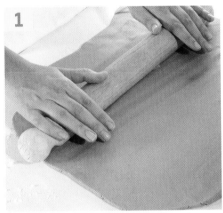

Using the rolling pin, roll out 30 oz (850 g) gray fondant into a sheet large enough to cover the entire cake.

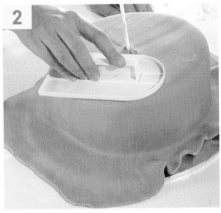

Slide the sheet down the balloon stick so it drapes over the cake. Use the cake smoother to smooth the top and sides of the cake. Trim off any excess fondant. Smooth again.

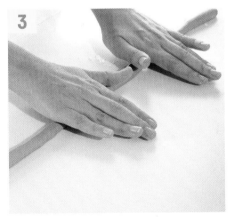

Using your hands, roll 5 oz (150 g) gray fondant into a thick tube long enough to wrap around the cake (about 25 inches/63 cm long).

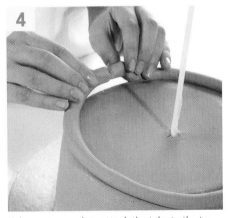

Using water as glue, attach the tube to the top of the cake, around the perimeter. Trim off any excess fondant and press the ends of the tube together. Loosely cover the cake with a kitchen towel and set in a cool spot.

TIPS

If you want to add a second layer of icing to the cake before applying the fondant, you will need an additional 1¾ cups (425 mL) icing for this recipe.

To prevent fondant from becoming sticky, dust your work surface with confectioners' (icing) sugar before working with it.

Loosely covering the cake with a clean kitchen towel at the end of step 4 prevents dust from falling on it while you are preparing and drying the handles. Alternatively, you could prepare the handles the day before you start this project.

If you don't have 24 hours to spare for the fondant handles to set, add CMC (Tylose powder) to the fondant before you make the handles and they will dry in about 4 hours.

5

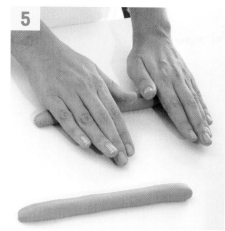

Divide the remaining gray fondant in half and, using your hands, roll each piece into a tube.

6

Bend each tube into a wide U shape. Trim off a little bit from both ends of each U to flatten the ends.

7

Place the U shapes on the parchment paper and slide a cake pop stick into both ends of each U. Let set for 24 hours to dry completely (see tip).

8

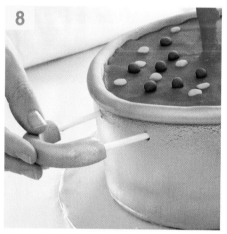

Dampen the cake pop sticks with water and slide the sticks into either side of the cake, near the top, so that the U shapes resemble handles.

9

Spray the entire cake with silver spray and let stand for 25 to 30 minutes or until dry.

10

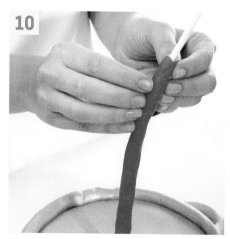

Working from the top down, mold the orange fondant around the portion of the balloon stick that will not be covered by the soup can. Bend the stick to a natural pouring angle.

Form the green fondant into about 15 balls the size of peas.

Form the yellow fondant into about 15 balls the size of corn kernels, then press on the sides to give the pieces a more squared shape.

In a small bowl, combine 4 drops red, 4 drops yellow and 2 drops orange food coloring with 2½ tbsp (37 mL) water. Thoroughly mix in royal icing mix. Spread most of this "soup" mixture over the top of your cake, inside the rim.

Arrange the peas and corn in the soup mixture while it's still wet.

Using the pastry brush, brush the remaining soup mixture over the fondant on the balloon stick.

Slide the can down the stick. If desired, place the spoon on the cake board for decoration.

TIPS

If desired, when the cake has dried after step 9, cover the cake board with 10 oz (300 g) brown fondant (see page 33) and press it all the way around with a wood-grain fondant impression mat.

In step 13, you are trying to create a mixture with a stiff liquid consistency; it shouldn't be too runny. Tweak the mixture with more royal icing mixture or water as needed.

CHEESEBURGER

The only thing better than a delicious cheeseburger is one that is made of cake and icing. This amazing cake design will be a showstopper at any party! Feeds 30.

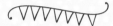

EQUIPMENT

- 8-inch (20 cm) round ovenproof bowl
- 2 balloon sticks
- 16-inch (40 cm) round cake board or wooden slab
- Six 18-gauge wires
- Clean, empty lightweight ketchup bottle
- Clean, empty lightweight mustard bottle
- Rolling pin
- Cake smoother
- Ball tool (optional)
- Pastry brush
- 8-inch (20 cm) thin round cake board

INGREDIENTS

- 2 tbsp (30 mL) candy coating wafers
- 2 cups (500 mL) vanilla butter icing
- 8-inch (20 cm) round vanilla cake, leveled
- Confectioners' (icing) sugar
- 40 oz (1.2 kg) cream fondant

GETTING STARTED

Melt the candy wafers, attach the balloon sticks about 3 inches (7.5 cm) apart in the center of the 16-inch (40 cm) cake board and let set. Spread a small dollop of vanilla icing around the base of each stick. Center the leveled vanilla cake above the cake board and slide the cake down the sticks. Crumb-coat the cake with vanilla icing. Slide three 18-gauge wires down inside each stick and trim the sticks and wires to the height of the ketchup and mustard bottles plus about 5 inches (12.5 cm) from the top of the cake.

Dust your work surface with sugar. Using the rolling pin, roll out 20 oz (575 g) cream fondant into a sheet large enough to cover the iced vanilla cake.

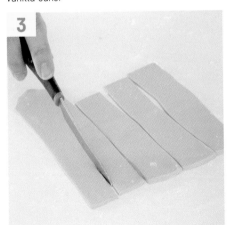

Slide the sheet down the balloon sticks so it drapes over the cake. Use the cake smoother to smooth the top and sides of the cake. Trim off any excess fondant. Smooth again.

Roll out the green fondant until very thin and smooth. Cut into strips about 6 inches (15 cm) long and 1¼ inch (3 cm) wide.

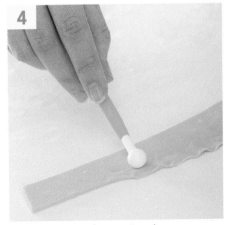

Using the ball tool (or your finger), create natural-looking crimps in the fondant strips, making them look like ruffled lettuce.

continued on next page

INGREDIENTS

- 4 oz (125 g) light green fondant
- Small bowl of water
- 1 cup (250 mL) chocolate butter icing
- 6-inch (15 cm) round chocolate cake, leveled
- 2 oz (60 g) yellow fondant
- Vanilla cake baked in ovenproof bowl (see tip)
- 2 oz (60 g) red fondant
- 2 oz (60 g) dark yellow (mustard) fondant
- Small round white sprinkles

TIPS

Fill the ovenproof bowl only three-quarters full with cake batter, to allow room for expansion.

Don't worry about making the chocolate icing look smooth and perfect; a little texture will make the cake look more like a burger patty.

If the bowl cake doesn't cover the 8-inch (20 cm) cake board completely, cut the board to ensure that it is hidden.

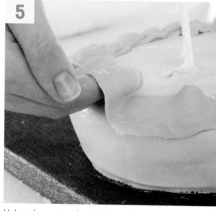

5

Using the pastry brush dipped in water, dampen a 1-inch (2.5 cm) border on top of the cake. Attach the crimped strips to the dampened border, extending them slightly over the edge of the cake. Overlap the strips so there are no gaps.

6

Spread some chocolate icing inside the lettuce circle. Center the chocolate cake over the lettuce circle and slide it down the sticks.

7

Crumb-coat the cake with chocolate icing (see tip), taking care not to get any chocolate on the lettuce.

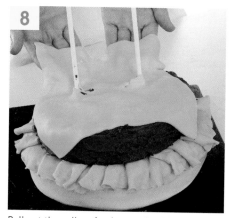

8

Roll out the yellow fondant to the thickness of a cheese slice and cut out a 7-inch (18 cm) square. Center the square over the chocolate cake and slide it down the sticks.

9

Slice across the bottom of the vanilla bowl cake to ensure it is completely flat. Spread some vanilla icing in the center of the 8-inch (20 cm) cake board and rest the cake on top (see tip).

10

Smother the bowl cake in vanilla icing, making the icing as smooth as possible. Refrigerate for 20 minutes.

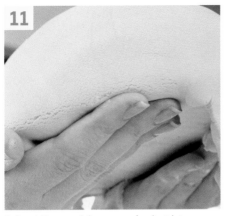

11

Roll out the remaining cream fondant into a sheet large enough to cover the bowl cake. Drape the sheet over the cake, wrapping it underneath the board. Smooth the cake and trim off any excess fondant.

12

Working from the top down, mold most of the red fondant around the portion of a balloon stick that will not be covered by the ketchup bottle. Bend the stick to a natural pouring angle.

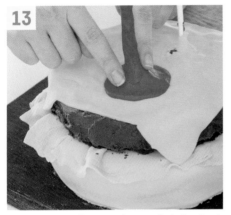

13

Using water as glue, attach a small circle of red fondant in a pool around the base of the stick.

14

Working from the top down, mold most of the dark yellow fondant around the portion of the other stick that will not be covered by the mustard bottle. Bend the stick to a natural pouring angle.

15

Using water as glue, attach a small circle of dark yellow fondant in a pool around the base of the stick. Slide the ketchup and mustard bottles down the sticks.

16

Using the pastry brush, dampen the entire surface of the bowl cake with water. Sprinkle the entire surface of the cake generously with white sprinkles. Carefully rest the bun top at an angle against the burger.

If you want to add a second layer of icing to the leveled vanilla cake and the bowl cake before applying the fondant, you will need an additional $1\frac{1}{4}$ cups (300 mL) vanilla icing for this recipe.

SPAGHETTI AND MEATBALLS

GETTING STARTED

Roll the brown fondant into eight 2-inch (5 cm) "meatballs" and place on the parchment paper to set for 12 hours (see tip, page 146). Melt the candy wafers, attach the balloon stick in the center of the display bowl and let set. Spread a small dollop of icing around the base of the stick. Center the cake over the bowl and slide the cake down the stick. Using a serrated knife, round the top edges of the cake into a dome, so it sits more nicely in the bowl. Crumb-coat the cake and refrigerate for 20 minutes. Fill the pastry bag with the remaining icing. Slide the 18-gauge wires down inside the stick and trim the stick and wires to the same height.

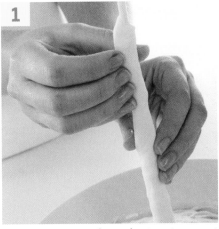

Starting about 1 inch (2.5 cm) below the top and working down, mold the white fondant around the balloon stick.

Pipe icing spaghetti all over the cake, filling all the gaps. Pipe spaghetti up and down the fondant on the balloon stick until the fondant is completely covered.

You'll love this sweet twist on a classic Italian meal.

Smother your cake in icing noodles and a mouthwatering strawberry jam sauce and take spaghetti and meatballs to the next level! Feeds 10.

EQUIPMENT

- Parchment paper
- Balloon stick
- Display bowl large enough to hold an 8-inch (20 cm) cake
- Serrated knife
- Pastry bag fitted with a #2 round tip
- Three 18-gauge wires
- Small paintbrush
- Lightweight plastic fork

INGREDIENTS

- 7 oz (200 g) brown fondant
- 1 tbsp (15 mL) candy coating wafers
- 1½ cups (375 mL) butter icing
- 8-inch (20 cm) round cake, leveled
- 2 oz (60 g) white fondant
- ¾ cup (175 mL) royal icing mix
- ¼ cup (60 mL) strawberry jam
- 5 drops red gel food coloring
- 2 drops brown gel food coloring

If you don't have 12 hours to spare for the meatballs to set, add CMC (Tylose powder) to the fondant before you make them and they will dry in about 4 hours.

If you want to add a second layer of icing to the cake, you will need an additional ⅔ cup (150 mL) for this recipe.

3

Arrange 7 meatballs on top of the spaghetti.

4

Using the paintbrush, brush the top of the balloon stick with water. Slide the remaining meatball down the balloon stick to the fondant. Push the tines of the plastic fork into the meatball on the stick.

5

In a small bowl, combine royal icing mix, jam, red food coloring, brown food coloring and 1 tbsp (15 mL) water. Pour this mixture all over the meatballs, including the one on the stick.

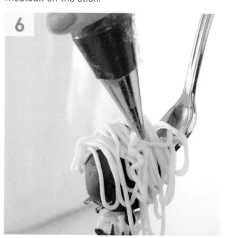

6

Pipe some spaghetti onto the meatball on the stick.

Buon appetito!

ASIAN NOODLES

GETTING STARTED

Melt the candy wafers, attach the balloon stick in the center of the bowl and let set. Spread a small dollop of icing around the base of the stick. Trim the first cake to fit nicely inside the bowl, then center it over the bowl and slide it down the stick. Cover the top with icing. Trim the second cake as needed, then center it over the bowl and slide it down the stick. Crumb-coat the entire cake. Slide the 18-gauge wires down inside the stick and trim the stick and wires to the same height.

EQUIPMENT

- Balloon stick
- 7-inch (18 cm) bowl
- Three 18-gauge wires
- 24 inches (60 cm) thin ribbon
- Lightweight chopsticks
- Rolling pin
- Pastry brush

INGREDIENTS

- 1 tbsp (15 mL) candy coating wafers
- 2 cups (500 mL) vanilla butter icing
- Two 7-inch (18 cm) round cakes, leveled
- 11 oz (325 g) cream fondant
- Confectioners' (icing) sugar
- Small bowl of water
- 1 oz (30 g) white fondant
- 1/8 oz (4 g) yellow fondant
- 1/8 oz (4 g) red fondant
- 1 oz (30 g) green fondant

Starting at the top and working down, mold 1 oz (30 g) cream fondant around the balloon stick. Bend the stick slightly.

Cut the ribbon in half. Use one piece to tie the chopsticks together near the narrow ends (see tip, page 150). Use the other piece to tie the chopsticks to the top of the balloon stick. Cut off excess ribbon.

Dust your work surface with sugar. Using the rolling pin, roll out the remaining cream fondant into a long rectangle. Cut into thin noodles slightly longer than the height of the balloon stick above the cake.

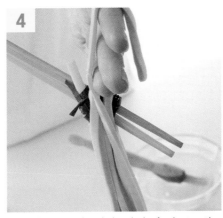

Using the pastry brush, brush the fondant on the balloon stick with water and attach the noodles to the stick (see tip, page 150). Trim off any remaining visible stick at the top.

TIPS

If you want to add a second layer of icing to the cake, you will need an additional 1 cup (250 mL) icing for this recipe.

In step 2, intertwine the ribbon between the chopsticks, wrapping it around them and tying multiple knots to make sure it holds firm.

In step 4, use the noodles to hide the ribbon at the top of the stick and around the chopsticks, and let them hang all the way down the stick to the surface of the cake, covering the fondant on the stick completely. You will need to keep dampening the noodles as you attach them.

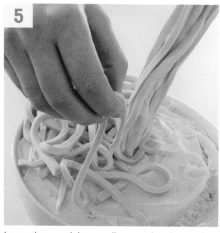

5 Layer the remaining noodles, overlapping each other, on top of the cake.

6 Form the white fondant into the loose, flat shape of a fried egg white. Form the yellow fondant into a dome shape and, using water as glue, attach it to the center of the egg white.

7 For the chile peppers, form the red fondant into a thick tube, then cut the tube crosswise into slices. Using the end of a paintbrush or pen, stamp a wide hole through the middle of each slice.

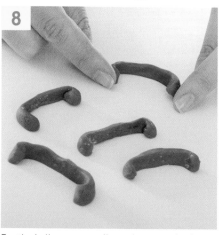

8 For the bell peppers, roll out the green fondant until smooth, then cut out strips the size of pepper slices. Curl up the ends of each strip.

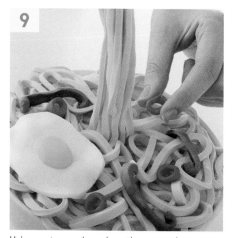

9 Using water as glue, place the egg and scatter the chile peppers and bell peppers on top of the noodles.

Your favorite noodle dish just got a lot sweeter!

CHERRY PIE WITH CUSTARD CREAM

Impress your friends with this amazing custard pie illusion! Feeds 10.

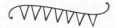

GETTING STARTED

Remove the cooled cake from the pie plate. Melt the candy wafers, attach the balloon stick to the center of the pie plate and let set. Spread a good amount of icing over the base of the plate. Center the cake over the stick and slide it down the stick back into the pie plate. Cover the top with icing. Slide the 18-gauge wires down inside the stick and trim the stick and wires to the height of the custard carton plus 7 inches (18 cm) from the top of the cake.

EQUIPMENT

- Deep-dish ceramic pie plate (about 7½ inches/19 cm wide and 2½ inches/6 cm deep) (see tip, page 154)
- Balloon stick
- Three 18-gauge wires
- Clean, empty small display custard carton (see tip, page 154)
- Rolling pin
- Pastry brush
- Small paintbrush

INGREDIENTS

- Cake baked in pie plate (see tip, page 154)
- 1 tbsp (15 mL) candy coating wafers
- 1¼ cups (300 mL) butter icing
- 7 oz (200 g) red fondant
- Confectioners' (icing) sugar
- Strawberry or raspberry jelly (or any red jelly)
- 8 oz (250 g) cream fondant
- Small bowl of water
- Brown gel food coloring
- 3 oz (90 g) light yellow fondant

Using 3 oz (90 g) red fondant, roll several loose, flattened balls with your hands (to represent cherries). Scatter them across the cake, leaving 1 inch (2.5 cm) clear around the border.

Dust your work surface with sugar. Using the rolling pin, roll out the remaining red fondant into a circle large enough to cover the cherries, trimming it to size as needed.

Bake your favorite cake and smother it with icing and delicious fondant.

TIPS

If you cannot find a pie plate without a rim in the correct size, a round casserole dish of the same size will work.

If you cannot locate a small display custard carton, try using a lightweight plastic jug or pouring utensil instead. Try toy shops and craft stores!

Before adding the cake batter to the pie plate, grease the bottom and sides of the plate and line the base with parchment paper. After the cake is baked and cooled, gently trim around the edges with a knife to ensure that it doesn't stick to the dish when you tip it out.

When cutting strips, use a clean plastic ruler to help you cut straight lines.

3

Slide the circle down the balloon stick to cover the cake, pressing it down to accentuate the cherries underneath. Brush the red fondant with red jelly until evenly glazed.

4

Using the rolling pin, roll out 5 oz (150 g) cream fondant into a 7-inch (18 cm) long, 5-inch (12.5 cm) wide rectangle. Use a sharp knife and a ruler to straighten the edges.

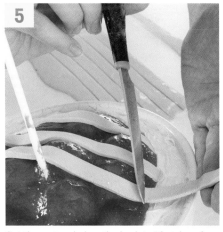

5

Cut the rectangle lengthwise into 10 strips of even width. One by one, place 5 strips across the red fondant, spacing them evenly and trimming the edges so they cover only the red fondant.

6

Lay the final 5 strips across the first to form a grid. Gently push the strips down to accentuate the cherries.

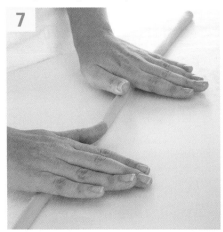

7

Using your hands, roll the remaining cream fondant into a tube long enough to wrap around the cake (about 25 inches/63 cm long).

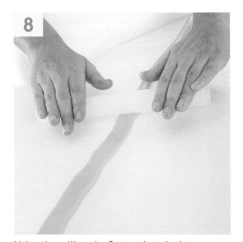

8

Using the rolling pin, flatten the tube into a 1-inch (2.5 cm) wide strip. (Don't flatten it too thin.) Use a sharp knife and a ruler to straighten the edges.

9

Using water as glue, gently attach the strip to the top of the cake, around the perimeter, letting it hang slightly over the sides. Trim off any excess fondant and press the ends of the strip together.

10

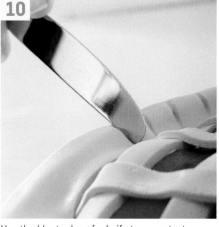

Use the blunt edge of a knife to score texture lines into the crust.

11

Mix 1 drop of brown food coloring and 10 drops of water (see tip). Using the paintbrush, lightly paint the food coloring over all the strips of cream fondant.

12

Working from the top down, mold 1½ oz (45 mL) yellow fondant around the portion of the stick that will not be covered by the custard carton. Bend the stick to a natural pouring angle.

13

Form most of the remaining yellow fondant into 4 loose splotches and arrange them on the cake around the bottom of the balloon stick.

14

Form the remaining fondant into small droplets and attach them to the cake and the stick to create a natural-looking drizzle. Slide the custard carton down the stick.

TIPS

If you want to add a second layer of icing to the top of the cake before applying the fondant, you will need an additional ⅔ cup (150 mL) icing for this recipe.

Before painting the strips in step 11, brush some of the food coloring onto excess cream fondant to ensure the color is diluted enough to create a natural-looking crust color.

BUCKET OF POPCORN

GETTING STARTED

Melt 1 tbsp (15 mL) candy wafers, attach the balloon stick to the center of the cake board and let set. Slide the 18-gauge wires down inside the stick and trim the stick and wires to the height of the paper bag plus about 5 inches (12.5 cm) from the top of the cake.

Stack all 4 cakes, adding a layer of icing between each layer.

Using a serrated knife, carve down along the sides of the cake in a gradual inward diagonal, creating a bucket shape.

Crumb-coat the cake, loosely cover it with a clean kitchen towel and set it aside to thaw completely, about 1 hour.

When the cake is thawed, spread a dollop of icing around the base of the balloon stick, center the cake over the stick and slide it down the stick.

This fun popcorn cake offers a simple design but a big effect that will make any party pop. Feeds 30.

EQUIPMENT

- Balloon stick
- 12-inch (30 cm) round cake board
- Three 18-gauge wires
- Small colorful paper bag
- Serrated knife
- Rolling pin
- Cake smoother
- Pastry brush

INGREDIENTS

- ½ cup (125 mL) white candy coating wafers
- Four 7-inch (18 cm) round cakes, leveled and frozen
- 20 oz (600 g) butter icing
- Confectioners' (icing) sugar
- 36 oz (1 kg) white fondant
- 6 oz (175 g) red fondant
- Small bowl of water
- 4 cups (1 L) popped popcorn

TIPS

If you want to add a second layer of icing to the cake before applying the fondant, you will need an additional 2⅓ cups (575 mL) icing for this recipe.

If there is any part of your cake where the red strips do not look symmetrical, simply make that side the back of the cake.

Dust your work surface with sugar. Using the rolling pin, roll out 30 oz (850 g) white fondant into a sheet large enough to cover the entire cake.

Slide the sheet down the balloon stick so it drapes over the cake. Use the cake smoother to smooth the top and sides of the cake. Trim off any excess fondant. Smooth again.

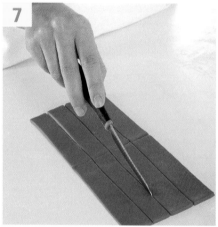

Using the rolling pin, roll out the red fondant until thin and smooth. Cut into strips that are 1 inch (2.5 cm) wide and slightly taller than the cake.

Using water as glue, attach a strip vertically to the side of the cake, draping it over the top.

Continue to attach strips, leaving gaps of equal distance between each strip, all the way around the cake (see tip).

Using your hands, roll 2 oz (60 g) white fondant into a tube long enough to wrap around the base of the cake. Using water as glue, gently wrap the tube around the base (see tip, page 161).

11

Roll 4 oz (125 g) white fondant into a tube long enough to wrap around the outer edges at the top of the cake. Using water as glue, gently wrap the tube around the top of the cake.

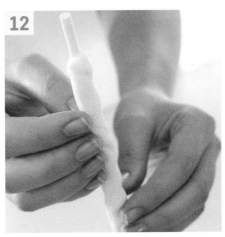

12

Starting near the top and working down, mold 2 oz (60 g) white fondant around the balloon stick.

13

Melt the remaining candy wafers and brush the top of the cake with melted candy. Place a layer of popcorn on top.

14

Add more layers of popcorn, using a dab of melted candy as glue on each piece, piling the popcorn nice and high and focusing it around the balloon stick. Attach popcorn to the fondant on the balloon stick.

15

Using melted candy as glue, attach popcorn here and there on the sides of the cake and on the cake board, to look as if it is overflowing from the bucket. Slide the paper bag down the stick.

TIPS

The red strips may push the white tubes around the base and top out a bit, making them look uneven. If so, gently push against them with the cake smoother.

If the melted candy starts to harden while you are working on attaching the popcorn pieces in steps 13 to 15, add a drop of vegetable oil and reheat.

In step 14, you can cover the fondant all the way up the balloon stick, if you like, but the paper bag will cover much of the top of the stick, so you really only need to conceal the fondant that will not be covered by the bag.

Bring the movie experience into your living room!

MUG OF BEER

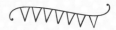

GETTING STARTED

Melt the candy wafers, attach the balloon stick to the center of the cake board and let set. Spread a small dollop of icing around the base of the stick. Center the first cake over the stick and slide it down the stick. Cover the top with icing. Repeat with the second and third cakes. Center and slide the fourth cake down the stick. Crumb-coat the entire cake. Slide the 18-gauge wires down inside the stick and trim the stick and wires to the height of the beer can plus about 5 inches (12.5 cm) from the top of the cake.

EQUIPMENT

- Balloon stick
- 12-inch (30 cm) round cake board
- Three 18-gauge wires
- Clean, empty beer can
- Rolling pin
- Cake smoother
- Table knife
- Small paintbrush
- 6-inch (15 cm) cake pop stick, cut in half

INGREDIENTS

- 1 tbsp (15 mL) candy coating wafers
- 7½ cups (1.875 L) vanilla butter icing (see tip)
- Four 7-inch (18 cm) round cakes, leveled
- Confectioners' (icing) sugar
- 32 oz (900 g) cream fondant
- Cream gel food coloring

TIP

Try using colorless vanilla extract instead of the more common brown extract to keep your icing very white in color; this will make the froth look better.

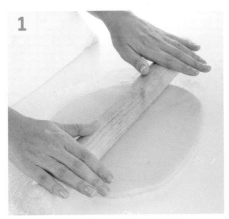

1 Dust your work surface with sugar. Using the rolling pin, roll out 28 oz (800 g) cream fondant into a sheet large enough to cover the entire cake.

2 Slide the sheet down the balloon stick so it drapes over the cake. Use the cake smoother to smooth the top and sides of the cake. Trim off any excess fondant. Smooth again.

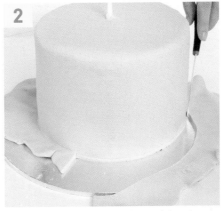

3 Gently press the flat side of the table knife vertically against the fondant on the side of the cake, about ½ inch (1 cm) from the bottom, and swipe up to the top, creating a groove.

4 Continue making grooves all the way around the cake, spacing them about 1 inch (2.5 cm) apart. Be careful not to pierce the fondant with the sharp edges of the knife.

TIPS

If you want to add a second layer of icing to the cake before applying the fondant, you will need an additional 2¼ cups (550 mL) icing for this recipe.

Before painting the grooves in step 6, brush some of the diluted food coloring onto excess cream fondant to make sure the color is correct. You want a caramel color.

Loosely covering the cake with a clean kitchen towel at the end of step 6 prevents dust from falling on it while you are preparing and drying the handle. Alternatively, you could prepare the handle the day before you start this project.

When rolling the handle for the beer mug in step 7, hold it up to the cake to make sure it's the right size and adjust as necessary.

If you don't have 24 hours to spare for the fondant handle to set, add CMC (Tylose powder) to the fondant before you make the handle and it will dry in about 4 hours.

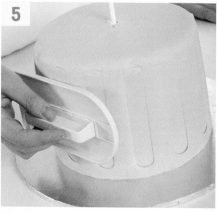

Slide the cake smoother up and down the sides of the cake to restore a flat, even surface in between the grooves.

In a small bowl, combine 3 drops cream food coloring and 3 drops water (see tip). Using the paintbrush, brush the food coloring inside the grooves. Loosely cover the cake with a kitchen towel and set in a cool spot.

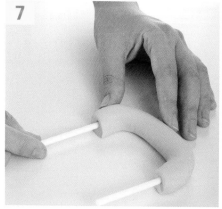

Roll 2 oz (60 g) cream fondant into a tube, then bend it to look like a beer mug handle (see tip). Trim the ends flat. Insert a cake pop stick half 1 inch (2.5 cm) deep into each end. Let set for 24 hours (see tip).

Dampen the fondant on the side of the cake where the handle will go. Dampen the cake pop sticks and slide the sticks into the dampened area on the cake to attach the mug handle.

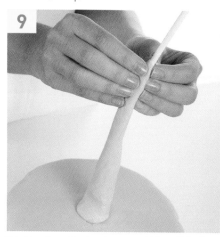

Working from the top down, mold 2 oz (60 g) cream fondant around the portion of the balloon stick that will not be covered by the beer can. Bend the stick to a natural pouring angle.

Slather the remaining icing on top of the cake and over the edges, to resemble froth. Slide the beer can down the stick.

POKER PARTY

Transport yourself to the Las Vegas strip with this delicious gambling-themed treat, complete with a mixed drink. Feeds 20.

GETTING STARTED

Melt the candy wafers, attach the balloon sticks 1 inch (2.5 cm) apart in the center of the cake board and let set. Spread a small dollop of icing around the base of each stick. Center the first cake over the cake board and slide it down the sticks. Cover the top with icing. Center and slide the second cake down the sticks. Crumb-coat the entire cake. Slide three 18-gauge wires down inside each stick. Trim one stick and its wires to the height of the soda can plus about 8 inches (20 cm) from the top of the cake. Trim the other stick and its wires to the height of the liquor bottle plus about 6 inches (15 cm) from the top of the cake.

EQUIPMENT

- 2 balloon sticks
- 12-inch (30 cm) round cake board
- Six 18-gauge wires
- Clean, empty soda can
- Clean, empty mini plastic liquor bottle
- Rolling pin
- Texture fondant impression mat
- Cake smoother
- Edible ink printer (see tip, page 169)
- Twelve 1½-inch (4 cm) poker chip images, 4 yellow, 4 blue and 4 red
- Ten 2- by 1½-inch (5 by 4 cm) playing card images
- 1½-inch (4 cm) circle cutter
- Small paintbrush
- Parchment paper
- Plastic tumbler

INGREDIENTS

- 2 tbsp (30 mL) candy coating wafers
- 2 cups (500 mL) butter icing
- Two 8-inch (20 cm) round cakes, leveled

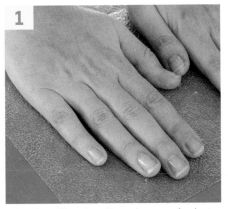

1 Using the rolling pin, roll out the green fondant into a sheet large enough to cover the entire cake. Press the sheet with the fondant impression mat.

2 Slide the sheet down the balloon stick so it drapes over the cake. Smooth the fondant (see tip, page 168) and trim off any excess. Loosely cover the cake with a kitchen towel and set in a cool spot.

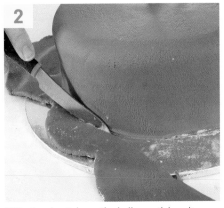

3 Using the edible ink printer, print the poker chip images on an edible frosting sheet and the playing card images on another frosting sheet. Cut out the poker chips and playing cards.

4 Roll out the yellow fondant to the thickness of a poker chip. Cut out 4 circles with the circle cutter.

continued on next page

INGREDIENTS

- 24 oz (700 g) green fondant
- Edible frosting sheets
- 3 oz (90 g) yellow fondant
- Small bowl of water
- 3 oz (90 g) blue fondant
- 3 oz (90 g) red fondant
- 7 oz (200 g) white fondant
- 7 oz (200 g) dark brown fondant
- 1 oz (30 g) caramel-colored fondant
- 3 tbsp (45 mL) royal icing mix

TIPS

If you want to add a second layer of icing to the cake before applying the fondant, you will need an additional 1¼ cups (300 mL) icing for this recipe.

To prevent fondant from becoming sticky, dust your work surface with confectioners' (icing) sugar before working with it.

Once you have smoothed the fondant, you may lose some of the texture from the impression mat. Gently press the mat onto the fondant again to enhance the effect.

If desired, after step 2 cover the cake board with 10 oz (300 g) brown fondant (see page 33).

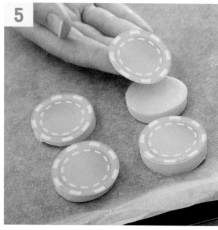

Using the paintbrush, brush the top of each fondant circle with water and attach a yellow poker chip frosting piece. Place the fondant poker chips on the parchment paper.

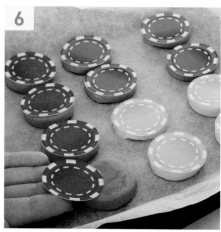

Repeat steps 4 and 5 with the blue fondant and blue poker chip pieces, and the red fondant and red poker chip pieces.

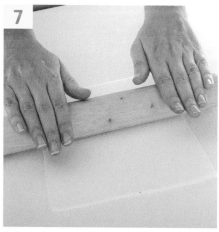

Roll out the white fondant into a rectangle slightly larger than 8 by 4 inches (20 by 10 cm), keeping it quite thick.

Brush the top of the rectangle with water and attach the playing card frosting pieces side by side on the fondant, being careful not to get them wet and smudge them.

Using a sharp knife, cut out the fondant cards and place them on the parchment paper. Let the chips and cards set for 24 hours (see tip, page 169).

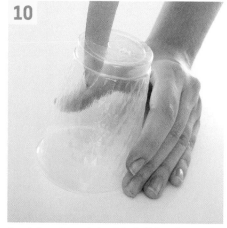

Carefully cut two holes 1 inch (2.5 cm) apart in the base of the plastic tumbler.

11

Dampen the top of the cake around the sticks with water and slide the cup down the sticks.

12

Drizzle some water inside the tumbler. Mound up 6 oz (175 g) brown fondant and slide it down the sticks into the cup. Gently mold the fondant to sit neatly in the cup.

13

Working from the top down, mold the remaining brown fondant around the portion of the taller balloon stick that will not be covered by the soda can.

14

Mold the caramel fondant around the portion of the other balloon stick that will not be covered by the liquor bottle. Bend the sticks away from each other to a natural pouring angle.

15

In a small bowl, combine royal icing mix and 2 tbsp (30 mL) water. Using this mixture as glue, attach the cards and chips to the cake (see tip).

16

Slide the soda can down the brown fondant stick and the liquor bottle down the caramel fondant stick.

TIPS

Loosely covering the cake with a clean kitchen towel prevents dust from falling on it while you are preparing and drying the cards and poker chips. Alternatively, you could prepare the cards and chips the day before you start this project.

To create the images for the poker chips and playing cards, search on the Internet for pictures that appeal to you, then use photo editing software to scale them to the specified size.

If you don't own an edible ink printer, you can order bespoke edible frosting sheets for playing cards and poker chips online, using the dimensions provided. Cut out the individual chips and cards and attach these cutouts to the fondant as instructed in steps 5, 6 and 8. Another option, if you want to design your own chips and cards, is to use an edible icing pen to draw your design directly on the fondant pieces.

If you don't have 24 hours to spare for the cards and chips to set, add CMC (Tylose powder) to the fondant before you make them and they will dry in about 4 hours.

BEACH PARTY

Get crafty by creating a beach ball and towel out of fondant with this easy, fun design! Feeds 20.

GETTING STARTED

Melt the candy wafers, attach the balloon stick to the center of the cake board and let set. Spread a small dollop of icing around the base of the stick. Center the first cake over the stick and slide it down the stick. Cover the top with icing. Center and slide the second cake down the stick. Crumb-coat the entire cake. Slide the 18-gauge wires down inside the stick and trim the stick and wires to the height of the bucket plus about 5 inches (12.5 cm) from the top of the cake.

EQUIPMENT

- Balloon stick
- 12-inch (30 cm) round cake board
- Three 18-gauge wires
- Mini display bucket
- Pastry brush
- Rolling pin
- 2-inch (5 cm) circle cutter
- Seashell fondant mold
- Cocktail umbrella

INGREDIENTS

- 1 tbsp (15 mL) candy coating wafers
- 2 cups (500 mL) butter icing
- Two 8-inch (20 cm) round cakes, leveled
- 7½ oz (215 g) white fondant
- 1 cup (250 mL) all-purpose flour
- ⅔ cup (150 mL) superfine sugar
- 7 tbsp (105 mL) butter, softened
- Small bowl of water
- ½ oz (15 g) blue fondant
- ½ oz (15 g) yellow fondant
- ¾ oz (23 g) red fondant
- 2 oz (60 g) green fondant

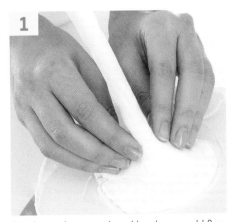

Starting at the top and working down, mold 2 oz (60 g) white fondant around the balloon stick. Mold 3 oz (90 g) fondant around the base of stick on top of the cake, creating a loose heap.

In a bowl, using your fingers, combine flour, sugar and butter until crumbly. Using the pastry brush, brush the fondant on the stick with water. Stick the crumble to the wet fondant, letting it fall onto the cake.

Sprinkle the remaining crumble over the top and around the sides of the cake (see tip, page 172).

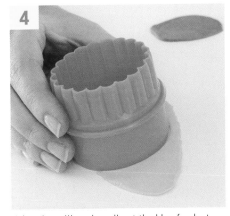

Using the rolling pin, roll out the blue fondant until smooth. Use the circle cutter to cut out a circle. Use half of the cutter to cut a long eye shape from the circle. Repeat with the yellow fondant and ½ oz (15 g) red fondant.

TIPS

If you want to add a second layer of icing to the cake before applying the fondant, you will need an additional 1¼ cups (300 mL) icing for this recipe.

To prevent fondant from becoming sticky, dust your work surface with confectioners' (icing) sugar before working with it.

If desired, before beginning step 1, cover the cake board with 10 oz (300 g) dark blue fondant marbled with white fondant, for a wave effect (pages 25 and 33).

In step 3, if the crumble isn't sticking to the icing on the sides of the cake, try spritzing the cake lightly with water.

5

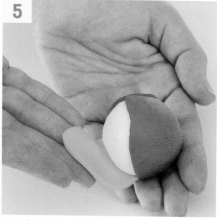

Roll 1½ oz (45 g) white fondant into a ball. Brush the ball with water and attach the colored fondant pieces vertically on different sides of the ball, leaving some space between them.

6

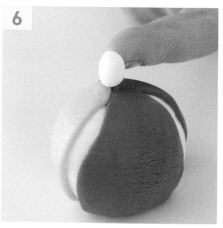

Form a tiny piece of white fondant into a flat circle and attach it on top of the beach ball to hide the seams. Place the ball on top of the cake.

7

Use the seashell mold to create a sea star with the remaining red fondant. Using water as glue, attach the sea star to the cake board, leaning against the cake.

8

Create 3 shells with white fondant and arrange them on the cake or attach them to the cake board.

9

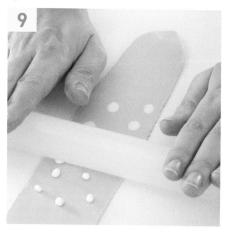

Roll out the green fondant into a thick strip. Roll tiny balls of white fondant and arrange them on the strip. Roll over the balls with a rolling pin until flattened into the green fondant. Cut the strip into a long rectangle.

10

Place the rectangle loosely on top of the cake, allowing it to wrinkle like a beach towel. Stick the umbrella into the cake next to the towel. Slide the bucket down the balloon stick.

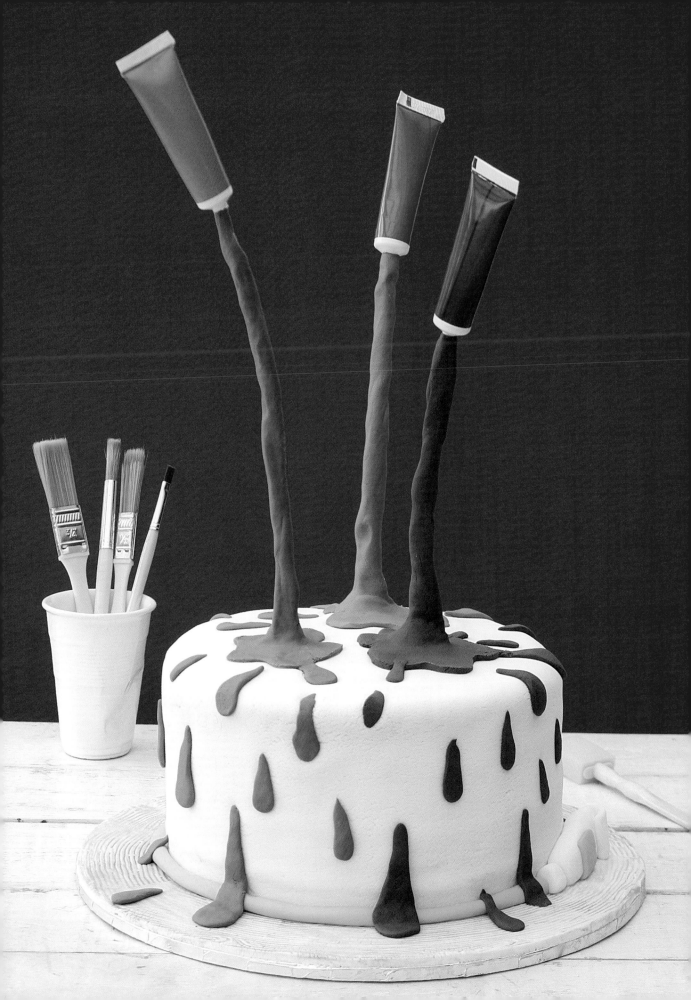

ARTIST'S PALETTE

Create a colorful masterpiece for an equally colorful friend, channeling your inner Picasso with this bright cake. Feeds 30.

EQUIPMENT

- 3 balloon sticks
- 12-inch (30 cm) round cake board
- Nine 18-gauge wires
- Rolling pin
- Cake smoother
- 3 small display paint tubes, 1 for green paint, 1 for red and 1 for purple

INGREDIENTS

- 3 tbsp (45 mL) candy coating wafers
- 3½ cups (875 mL) butter icing
- Four 8-inch (20 cm) round cakes, leveled
- Confectioners' (icing) sugar
- 31 oz (900 g) white fondant
- 2 oz (60 g) green fondant
- 2 oz (60 g) red fondant
- 1½ oz (45 g) purple fondant
- Small bowl of water
- 3 oz (90 g) yellow fondant

GETTING STARTED

Melt the candy wafers and attach the balloon sticks to the center of the cake board, forming the points of a triangle about 3½ inches (9 cm) apart. Let set. Spread a small dollop of icing around the base of each stick. Center the first cake over the cake board and slide it down the sticks. Cover the top with icing. Repeat with the second and third cakes. Center and slide the fourth cake down the sticks. Crumb-coat the entire cake. Slide three 18-gauge wires down inside each stick and trim the stick and wires to the same height.

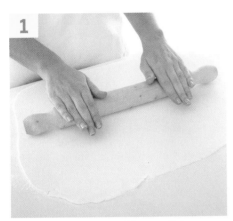

Dust your work surface with sugar. Using the rolling pin, roll out 30 oz (850 g) white fondant into a sheet large enough to cover the entire cake.

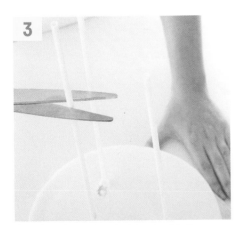

Slide the sheet down the balloon sticks so it drapes over the cake. Use the cake smoother to smooth the top and sides of the cake. Trim off any excess fondant and add it to the remaining white fondant. Smooth again.

Turn the cake so that the triangle of balloon sticks points down toward you. Trim 1 inch (2.5 cm) off the right-hand stick, and trim 2 inches (5 cm) off the stick closest to you. Slide a paint tube down each stick.

Working from the top down, mold 1 oz (30 g) green fondant around the stick with the green tube. Bend the stick outward to a natural pouring angle.

TIPS

If you want to add a second layer of icing to the cake before applying the fondant, you will need an additional 2½ cups (625 mL) icing for this recipe.

For the fondant paint tube, form most of the fondant into a long rectangular tube. Flatten one end very thin and roll it up toward the fat end. Flatten a marble-size piece of fondant into a thick disc and, using water as glue, attach it as the tube cap.

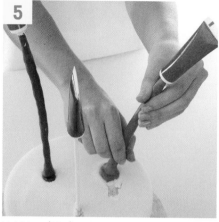

Mold 1 oz (30 g) red fondant around the stick with the red tube. Bend the stick outward to a natural pouring angle.

Mold ½ oz (15 g) purple fondant around the stick with the purple tube.

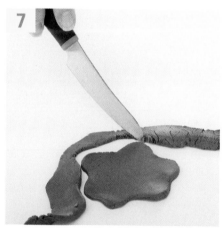

Roll out the remaining purple fondant until thin and smooth. Cut out a loose splotch shape. Set the excess fondant aside.

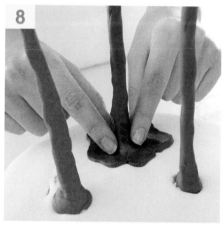

Cut a slit halfway down the middle of the splotch shape and place it around the purple balloon stick on top of the cake, molding it into place and blending the seam with your fingers.

Repeat steps 8 and 9 with the remaining red fondant and the remaining green fondant.

Form the remaining white fondant into the shape of a small paint tube (see tip). Using water as glue on the cake and cake board, place the paint tube on its side, leaning against the cake.

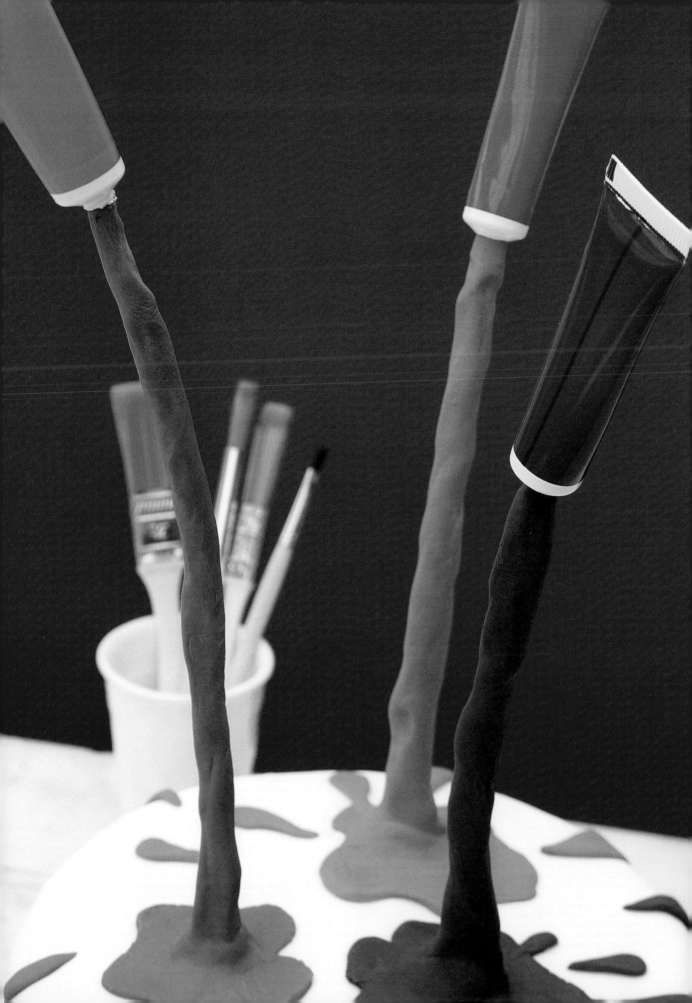

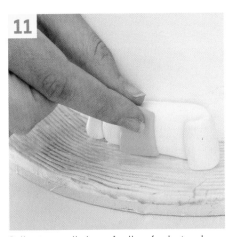

11

Roll out a small piece of yellow fondant and cut out a small square. Using water as glue, attach it to the front of the fondant paint tube, as a label.

12

Roll the remaining yellow fondant into a thin tube long enough to wrap all the way around the base of the cake from the fondant paint tube's cap to its rolled end.

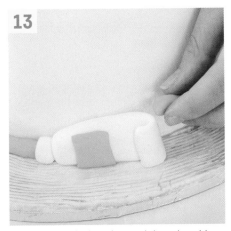

13

Dampen the cake board around the cake with water and wrap the yellow tube around the base of the cake, connecting it to the fondant paint tube at both ends.

14

Form the excess green, red and purple fondant into the shape of paint drops. Using water as glue, attach them to the top and sides of the cake, and the cake board, as if they are dripping from the splotches.

TIP

If desired, after step 2 cover the cake board with 10 oz (300 g) white fondant (see page 33), press it all the way around with a wood-grain fondant impression mat and paint it with silver edible paint.

Add a stroke of genius to your celebration with this simple yet beautiful design!

TOY BOX

Make a kid's birthday party the event of the year with this jaw-dropping toy box gravity cake! Feeds 40.

GETTING STARTED

Use the brick mold to form bricks from the blue, green, red and 10 oz (300 g) yellow fondant. Place the bricks on the prepared baking sheet and refrigerate for 24 to 48 hours (see tip, page 182). Melt 1 tbsp (15 mL) candy wafers, attach the balloon stick to the center of the cake board and let set. Spread a small dollop of icing around the base of the stick. Center the first cake over the cake board and slide it down the stick. Cover the top with icing. Repeat with the second and third cakes. Center and slide the fourth cake down the stick. Crumb-coat the entire cake. Slide the 18-gauge wires down inside the stick and trim the stick and wires to the height of the cardboard box plus about 5 inches (12.5 cm) from the top of the cake.

EQUIPMENT

- Building brick (such as Lego) fondant mold
- Baking sheet, lined with parchment paper
- Balloon stick
- 12-inch (30 cm) round cake board
- Three 18-gauge wires
- Small cardboard toy box
- Rolling pin
- Cake smoother
- 1½-inch (4 cm) and 1-inch (2.5 cm) circle cutters (optional)

INGREDIENTS

- 10 oz (300 g) blue fondant
- 10 oz (300 g) green fondant
- 10 oz (300 g) red fondant
- 45 oz (1.3 kg) yellow fondant
- ¾ cup (175 mL) candy coating wafers
- 2½ cups (625 mL) butter icing
- Four 8-inch (20 cm) round cakes, leveled (see tip, page 182)
- Small bowl of water
- 2 oz (60 g) black fondant
- 3 oz (90 g) white fondant

1 Divide the remaining yellow fondant in half. Using the rolling pin, roll out each half into a wide strip about 13 inches (33 cm) long.

2 Measure the height of the cake and add 1 inch (2.5 cm); trim the strips to that height.

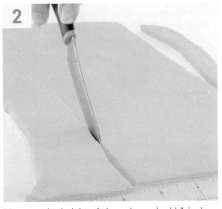

3 Brush the sides of the cake with water and gently wrap each strip around the cake, trimming off any excess at the seams. Smooth the fondant with the cake smoother.

4 Roll out the black fondant and 1 oz (30 g) white fondant. Using the circle cutters and/or a knife, cut out eyes, eyebrows and a smile (see tip, page 182).

TIPS

Before baking your cakes, add gel food coloring to the batter, making one red, one orange, one yellow and one green cake.

The longer you let the fondant bricks set, the sturdier they'll be. They'll be fairly strong after 24 hours, but 48 hours is ideal. If needed, you can speed up the process by adding CMC (Tylose powder) to the fondant.

If you want to add a second layer of icing to the cake before applying the fondant, you will need an additional 3 cups (750 mL) icing for this recipe.

To prevent fondant from becoming sticky, dust your work surface with confectioners' (icing) sugar before working with it.

In step 4, the circle cutters will help you create perfectly round eyes, but you can also cut them out free-hand.

When attaching the bricks in step 8, take your time and give each one time to set before adding another above it. If the melted candy starts to harden, add a drop of vegetable oil and reheat.

5 Turn the cake so the fondant seams are on the sides. Using water as glue, attach the features to the front of the cake.

7 Slide the cardboard toy box down the stick, making sure the front is featured.

9 Cover the top of the cake with fondant bricks until the icing is no longer visible.

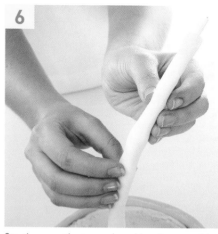

6 Starting near the top and working down, mold the remaining white fondant around the balloon stick. Bend the stick to a natural pouring angle.

8 Melt the remaining candy wafers. Using the melted candy as glue, attach fondant bricks to the fondant on the balloon stick, covering it all the way up to the toy box (see tip).

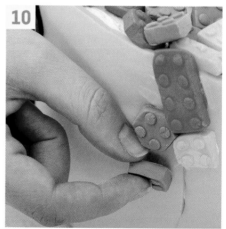

10 Using the melted candy as glue, attach bricks to the cake board and to the sides of the cake, covering the seams in the fondant, so the bricks appear to be spilling out onto the cake board.

ADVANCED CAKES

ICE CREAM BIRTHDAY CAKE

The ultimate birthday cake to take your party to the next level, this four-layer extravaganza is overflowing with treats and filled with delicious butter icing. Feeds 45.

GETTING STARTED

Spread some icing on the 12-inch (30 cm) cake board where the cake will sit, to prevent it from sliding. Place one 8-inch (20 cm) cake in the center of the board and cover the top with icing. Place the other 8-inch cake on top. Crumb-coat the entire cake.

EQUIPMENT

- 12-inch (30 cm) round cake board
- Rolling pin
- Cake smoother
- 3 hollow plastic support dowels (¾ inch/2 cm wide)
- Pastry brush
- 7-inch (18 cm) thin round cake board

INGREDIENTS

- 3¾ cups (925 mL) butter icing
- Two 8-inch (20 cm) round cakes, leveled
- Confectioners' (icing) sugar
- 24 oz (700 g) pink fondant (see tip, page 188)
- 4 ice cream cones
- 4 oz (125 g) green fondant
- 4 oz (125 g) yellow fondant
- 8 oz (250 g) white fondant
- Small bowl of water
- 1 cup (250 mL) colored sprinkles

Dust your work surface with sugar. Using the rolling pin, roll out the pink fondant into a sheet large enough to cover the entire cake. Drape the sheet over the cake, smooth the fondant and trim off any excess. Smooth again.

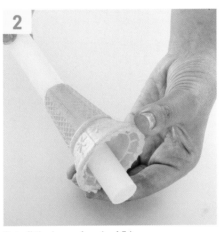

Stand 1 cone loosely on the cake and measure from the cake board to the top of the cone. Add 1½ inches (4 cm) to that height and make a note of the total.

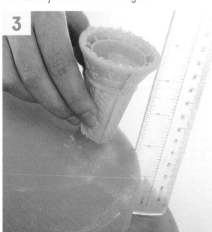

Cut off the base of each of 3 ice cream cones, making holes wide enough for the dowels to slide through. (Make sure the cones are all the same height.)

Cut each dowel to the noted measurement, being careful to cut a perfectly level edge.

continued on next page

INGREDIENTS

- Two 7-inch (18 cm) round cakes, leveled
- 21 oz (600 g) purple fondant
- 3 tbsp (45 mL) royal icing mix
- ½ cup (125 mL) milk chocolate candy coating wafers
- Assorted candies for decoration

TIPS

Vary the fondant colors as much as you like, using your favorite colors (or those of the person you are celebrating).

If you want to add a second layer of icing to the cakes before applying the fondant, you will need an additional 2½ cups (625 mL) icing for this recipe.

Placing the 7-inch (18 cm) cake on top of an upside-down bowl (or a tall glass) makes it easier to drape the fondant over the cake, trim the sides and add the sprinkles. To make cleanup easy, set the bowl on top of parchment paper, which will catch any sprinkles that fall so you can easily round them up.

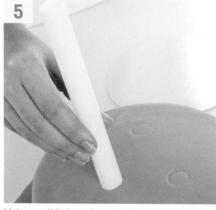

5 Make small indents in a triangle on the top of the cake to mark where the cones will sit, making sure the triangle is centered and will lie fully underneath the 7-inch (18 cm) cake to be placed above it.

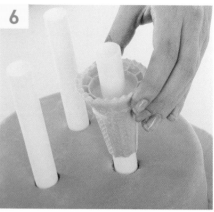

6 Slide the dowels into the marked indents on the cake, pushing them all the way down to the cake board. Slide the ice cream cones down the dowels, pushing them slightly into the cake to secure them.

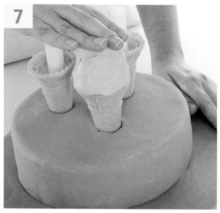

7 Roll the green fondant into a ball. Slide the ball down one of the dowels so it sits neatly on the cone and covers the dowel completely. Use your palm and fingers to flatten the top of the ball, making it level.

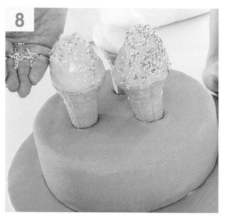

8 Repeat step 7 with the yellow fondant and 4 oz (125 g) white fondant. Dampen all 3 scoops with water and coat the sides with some of the sprinkles.

9 Spread some icing on the 7-inch (18 cm) cake board. Place one 7-inch cake in the center of the board and cover the top with icing. Place the final cake on top. Place the cake on an upside-down bowl (see tip). Crumb-coat the entire cake.

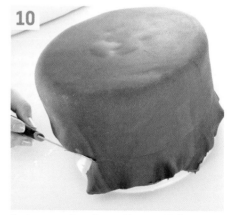

10 Dust your work surface with sugar. Roll out the purple fondant into a sheet large enough to cover the cake. Drape the sheet over the cake, smooth the fondant and trim off any excess below the cake board. Smooth again.

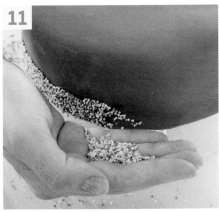

11 Using the pastry brush, brush water in a wide strip around the base of the small cake. Pat sprinkles all over the dampened area.

12 In a small bowl, combine royal icing mix and 2 tsp (10 mL) water. Reserve 1 tsp (5 mL) of the mixture. Add a dollop of the remaining mixture on top of each ice cream scoop to act as glue.

Use a wet pastry brush to wipe off any royal icing mixture that spills onto your cake.

In step 14, the shape you are forming is intended to look like a melting ice cream scoop, so don't worry about making it perfect.

If desired, after step 1 cover the cake board with 10 oz (300 g) fondant in a color that complements your cake (see page 33).

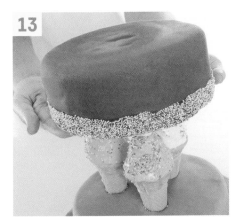

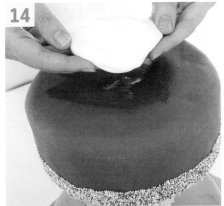

13 Rest the small cake on the ice cream scoops, centering it over the large cake.

14 Form the remaining white fondant into a loose scoop shape with a flat base (see tip). Dampen the center of the small cake with water and place the scoop on top.

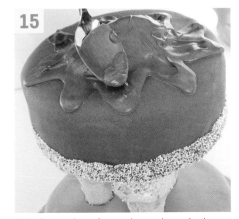

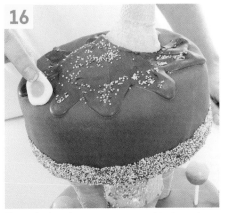

15 Melt the candy wafers and pour the melted chocolate over the scoop, using the back of a spoon to guide it over the top of the cake and slightly down the sides, to look like splattered ice cream.

16 Place the last ice cream cone upside down in the melted chocolate. Cover the chocolate with sprinkles. Decorate the cake and cake board with candies as desired, using the reserved icing mixture as glue.

CHAMPAGNE ON ICE

GETTING STARTED

Stack the 4 frozen cakes, smothering icing between each layer. Using a serrated knife, carve down along the sides of the bottom cake to create a bucket shape (see tip, page 194). Crumb-coat the cake, loosely cover it with a clean kitchen towel and set it aside to thaw completely, about 1 hour. Meanwhile, melt the candy wafers, attach the balloon stick to the center of the cake board and let set. When the cake is thawed, spread a dollop of icing around the base of the balloon stick, center the cake over the stick and slide it down the stick. Slide the 18-gauge wires down inside the stick and trim the wires to the height of the stick (see tip, page 194).

1

Dust your work surface with sugar. Using the rolling pin, roll out 35 oz (1 kg) gray fondant into a sheet large enough to cover the entire cake.

2

Slide the sheet down the balloon stick so it drapes over the cake. Use the cake smoother to smooth the top and sides of the cake. Trim off any excess fondant. Smooth again.

3

Roll 4 oz (125 g) gray fondant into a tube long enough to wrap around the outer edges at the top of the cake. Using water as glue, gently wrap the tube around the top of the cake.

4

Roll 2 oz (60 g) gray fondant into a tube long enough to wrap around the base of the cake. Using water as glue, gently wrap the tube around the base.

Whether it's a bridal shower or a birthday party, bring the most popular gift by creating this exploding Champagne bottle, complete with ice mints! Feeds 35.

EQUIPMENT

- Serrated knife
- Balloon stick
- 12-inch (30 cm) round cake board
- Three 18-gauge wires
- Rolling pin
- Cake smoother
- Silver edible spray paint
- Baking sheet lined with parchment paper
- Small paintbrush
- Gold edible paint
- 1-inch (2.5 cm) circle cutter

INGREDIENTS

- Five 7-inch (18 cm) round cakes, leveled and 4 cakes frozen
- 3 cups (750 mL) butter icing
- 1 tbsp (15 mL) candy coating wafers
- Confectioners' (icing) sugar
- 43 oz (1.2 kg) light gray fondant
- Small bowl of water
- 8 oz (250 g) dark green fondant

continued on next page

INGREDIENTS

- 1 oz (30 g) white fondant
- 3 oz (90 g) black fondant
- ½ oz (15 g) red fondant
- 1½ oz (45 g) brown fondant
- 1 oz (30 g) cream fondant
- 14 oz (425 g) clear mints

TIPS

You may want to carve down along the sides of more than just the bottom cake to create your ideal shape. If so, start by carving the bottom 2 cakes; carve the other cakes only as necessary.

The wires will add support to the stick while you build the cake, but you won't know the exact height you want the stick and wires to be until you add the cork right at the end. If you wish to trim the stick a bit as you get started, make sure you don't cut off too much!

Loosely covering the cake with a clean kitchen towel at the end of step 7 prevents dust from falling on it while you are preparing and chilling the bottle.

5 For each of 2 handles, roll 1 oz (30 g) gray fondant into a 5-inch (12.5 cm) long tube. Slice a small piece off each end to create flat edges.

6 Using water as glue, press the ends of each tube together to form a circle. Form the small fondant pieces you sliced off into two flat strips. Wrap each strip around the seam of a circle.

7 Using water as glue, attach the handles on opposite sides of the cake, near the top. Spray the entire cake with silver spray, let dry for 25 to 30 minutes, then loosely cover the cake with a kitchen towel and set in a cool spot.

8 Place the remaining cake in a large bowl and crumble into fine crumbs (or use an electric mixer to beat to fine crumbs).

9 Gradually add icing, 1 tbsp (15 mL) at a time, mixing it with the cake crumbs until the mixture is the consistency of a soft dough (see tip, page 195).

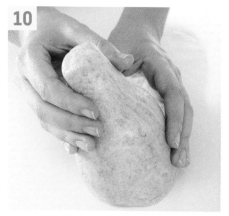

10 Using your hands, form the cake mixture into a shape that looks like the top half of a Champagne bottle without most of its neck. The bottle shape should appear to be resting at an angle (see tip, page 195).

11

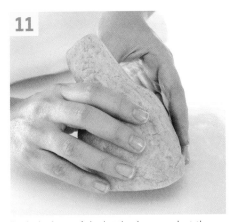

Push the base of the bottle shape against the work surface to make sure it is flat. Place it on the prepared baking sheet and refrigerate for at least 3 hours, until the mixture hardens and holds its shape.

12

Spread a thin layer of icing over the chilled bottle. Roll out the green fondant into a sheet large enough to cover the bottle. Mold the fondant over the bottle, trimming off and reserving excess fondant, and blend the seam together.

13

Dampen the area of the cake where the bottle will sit. Center the bottle over the balloon stick and guide the bottle down along the stick (see tip, page 196). Smooth out any creases in the fondant.

14

Roll the excess green fondant into a cylinder the same diameter as the top. Dampen the top of the bottle and slide the cylinder down the stick (see tip, page 196). Blend the seam. Pull out the top edges of the cylinder to look like a bottle rim.

15

Roll out the white fondant into a strip about 2 inches (5 cm) wide and long enough to wrap around the bottle neck. Dampen the bottleneck, wrap the white strip around it and blend the seam.

16

Pull down the edges at the top of the white fondant to create a crimped, ripped effect. Using the paintbrush, paint the white fondant with gold paint.

TIPS

If desired, when the cake has dried after step 7, cover the cake board with 10 oz (300 g) brown fondant (see page 33) and press it all the way around with a wood-grain fondant impression mat.

To ensure that your mixture is the right consistency in step 9, roll a small piece into a ball in your palm. If the mixture does not crumble, it is ready to go. Add more icing if it crumbles.

You want the bottle to look like it's leaning against the bucket, so in step 10, mold it to appear as if it's resting at an angle, using the pictures as a guide. Place it on the cake to make sure you are happy with the shape and size, and adjust as needed.

TIPS

In step 13, hold the bottle shape over the balloon stick as if the bottle were standing perfectly upright instead of at a slant. Slide the bottle in this position straight down the stick until one edge of the bottle touches the cake, then gradually tilt the bottle into its resting position while guiding the stick so it bends and remains in the center of the bottle.

If you find you had too much leftover green fondant and the bottle neck looks disproportionate after you join it with the bottle in step 14, slide it back up the stick and adjust it until you're satisfied.

Roll out the black fondant into a strip about 1 inch (2.5 cm) wide and 10 inches (25 cm) long. Use a sharp knife and a ruler to straighten the edges.

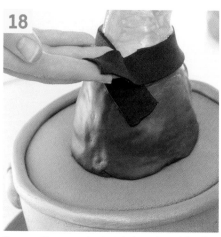

Dampen the green fondant below the gold strip and wrap the black strip around the bottle like a scarf, covering the bottom of the gold strip and crossing the ends of the black strip.

Roll out the red fondant until thin and smooth. Using the circle cutter, cut out a red circle. Using water as glue, attach the circle to the black strip at the point where the ends cross.

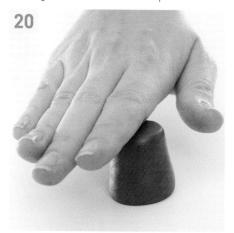

Roll 1 oz (30 g) brown fondant into a cylinder the same diameter as the bottle neck at the bottom and slightly tapered at the top. Gently push the ends of the cylinder against a flat surface.

Roll the remaining brown fondant into a thick circle that is slightly larger in diameter than the top of the cylinder. Using water as glue, attach the circle to the top of the cylinder.

Using a fork, poke holes all over the brown fondant to create a cork texture.

23

Hold the cork above the bottle rim and note the height above the bottle where you want the bottom of the cork to rest (it should look like it has just popped out of the bottle).

24

Working from the top down, mold half of the cream fondant around the stick up to the point where the bottom of the cork will rest.

TIP

If you want to add a second layer of icing to the cake before applying the fondant, you will need an additional 2½ cups (625 mL) icing for this recipe.

25

Use the remaining cream fondant to form small droplet shapes. Using water as glue, attach the droplets to the cream fondant on the stick, making sure they appear to be flying upward.

26

Trim the stick and wires slightly shorter than the height of the cork and slide the cork down the stick.

27

Using water as glue, arrange the mints on top of the cake, around the bottle, until the silver fondant is covered, allowing them to fall in different directions.

What better way to celebrate than with this amazing cake, filled with your favorite flavors!

JUST WHAT THE DOCTOR ORDERED

Help the medicine go down with a slice of this delicious cake! Feeds 20.

GETTING STARTED

Melt 1 tbsp (15 mL) candy wafers, attach the balloon stick to the center of the cake board and let set. Spread a small dollop of icing around the base of the stick. Center the first cake over the stick and slide it down the stick. Cover the top with icing. Center and slide the second cake down the stick. Crumb-coat the entire cake. Slide the 18-gauge wires down inside the stick and trim the stick and wires to the height of the pill bottle plus about 7 inches (18 cm) from the top of the cake.

EQUIPMENT

- Balloon stick
- 12-inch (30 cm) round cake board
- Three 18-gauge wires
- Empty display pill bottle
- Rolling pin
- Cake smoother
- ½-inch (1 cm) circle cutter
- Parchment paper
- Small paintbrush

INGREDIENTS

- ½ cup (125 mL) white candy coating wafers
- 2 cups (500 mL) butter icing
- Two 8-inch (20 cm) round cakes, leveled
- Confectioners' (icing) sugar
- 24 oz (700 g) light blue fondant
- ½ oz (15 g) cream fondant
- 3 oz (90 g) white fondant
- Small bowl of water
- 3¼ oz (100 g) black fondant
- 3 oz (90 g) gray fondant
- Silver edible paint
- ⅛ oz (4 g) yellow fondant
- ⅛ oz (4 g) red fondant

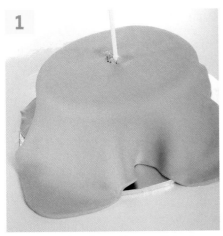

Dust your work surface with sugar. Using the rolling pin, roll out the blue fondant into a sheet large enough to cover the entire cake. Slide the sheet down the balloon stick so it drapes over the cake. Smooth the fondant and trim off any excess. Smooth again.

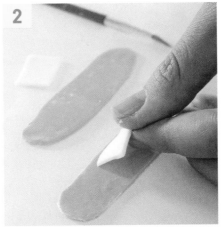

Divide the cream fondant in half and, using the rolling pin, roll out each piece into a long oval. Trim the pieces into the shape of adhesive bandages. Roll out a small piece of white fondant and cut out 2 small squares. Using water as glue, place one square in the center of each adhesive bandage.

Prescribe a double dose of oozing icing and decorate with fondant bandages and pills.

TIPS

If you want to add a second layer of icing to the cake before applying the fondant, you will need an additional 1¼ cups (300 mL) icing for this recipe.

If desired, after step 1 cover the cake board with 10 oz (300 mL) white fondant (see page 33).

Lightly cover the cake with a clean kitchen towel at the end of step 3 to prevent dust from falling on it while you are preparing and drying the pills. Alternatively, you could prepare the pills the night before you start this project.

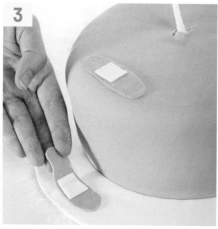

3 Using water as glue, place one adhesive bandage on the cake and the other on the cake board. Loosely cover the cake with a kitchen towel and set in a cool spot (see tip).

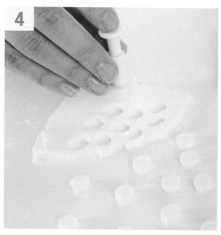

4 Using the rolling pin, roll out 2 oz (60 g) white fondant into a thick strip. Using the circle cutter, cut out as many pills as possible (see tip, page 203).

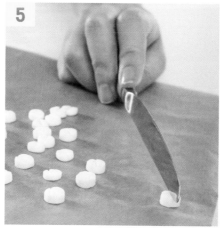

5 Use the blunt side of a knife to imprint a line down the center of each pill. Place pills on parchment paper and let set for at least 12 hours to dry completely (see tips, page 203).

6 Uncover the cake. Starting from the top and working down, mold the remaining white fondant around the stick. Bend the top of the stick slightly.

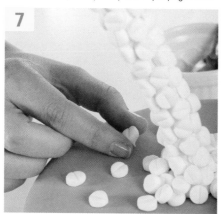

7 Melt the remaining candy wafers and, using the candy as glue, gently attach the pills to the fondant on the stick, up to the point where the bottom of the pill bottle will rest, and in a spreading pile around the base of the stick.

8 Using your hands, roll 2 oz (60 g) black fondant into a tube long enough to wrap halfway around the cake (about 12.5 inches/32 cm).

9

Roll the remaining black fondant into a tube the same width as the previous tube. Bend this tube into a wide U shape.

10

Using water as glue, attach the long tube to the bottom of U shape and blend the seams together with your fingers. Slice off about 1 inch (2.5 cm) from the end of each side of the U.

11

Divide 2 oz (60 g) gray fondant in half and, using your hands, roll each piece into a tube the same width as the U.

12

Using water as glue, attach a gray tube to each side of the U, blending the seams. Bend the gray tubes to resemble the earpieces of a stethoscope.

13

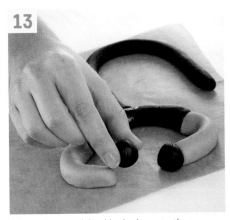

Attach the remaining black pieces to the open end of each gray tube, blending the seams. Place stethoscope on parchment paper.

14

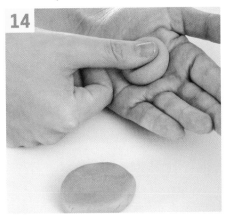

Form the remaining gray fondant into 2 balls, one slightly larger than the other (see tip, page 204). Flatten the larger ball a bit, keeping it as thick as possible. Push your thumb into the center of the other ball to create a groove.

TIPS

To get the most pills out of your fondant, keep rerolling it.

Don't push too hard with the knife when imprinting the line on the pills; a gentle, subtle line will create a natural look.

If you don't have 12 hours to spare for the fondant pills to set, add CMC (Tylose powder) to the fondant before you make the pills and they will dry in about 4 hours.

TIPS

When making the stethoscope pieces in step 14, you may not need to use all of the remaining gray fondant. Make the pieces proportionate with the rest of the stethoscope, removing a little bit of fondant as necessary.

To prevent fondant from becoming sticky, dust your work surface with confectioners' (icing) sugar before working with it.

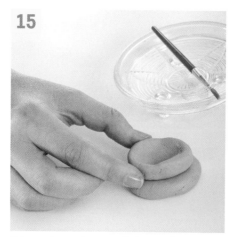

Using water as glue, attach the smaller gray piece to a flat side on the larger one. Place on parchment paper.

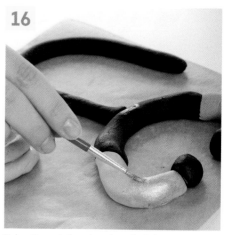

Using the paintbrush, paint all of the gray fondant pieces with silver paint and let dry for 25 to 30 minutes.

Place the top of the stethoscope on top of the cake, allowing the long black tube to dangle down the side and wrap around the cake board.

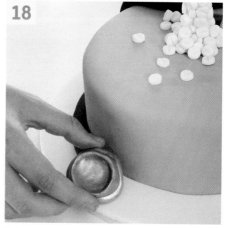

Using water as glue, attach the round silver base to the end of the tube on the cake board.

Form the yellow fondant into 5 small cylinders. Repeat with the red fondant, making all the cylinders as equal in size as possible. Gently push each yellow piece against a red piece to create capsules.

Using water as glue, attach the capsules to the cake board. Slide the pill bottle down the balloon stick.

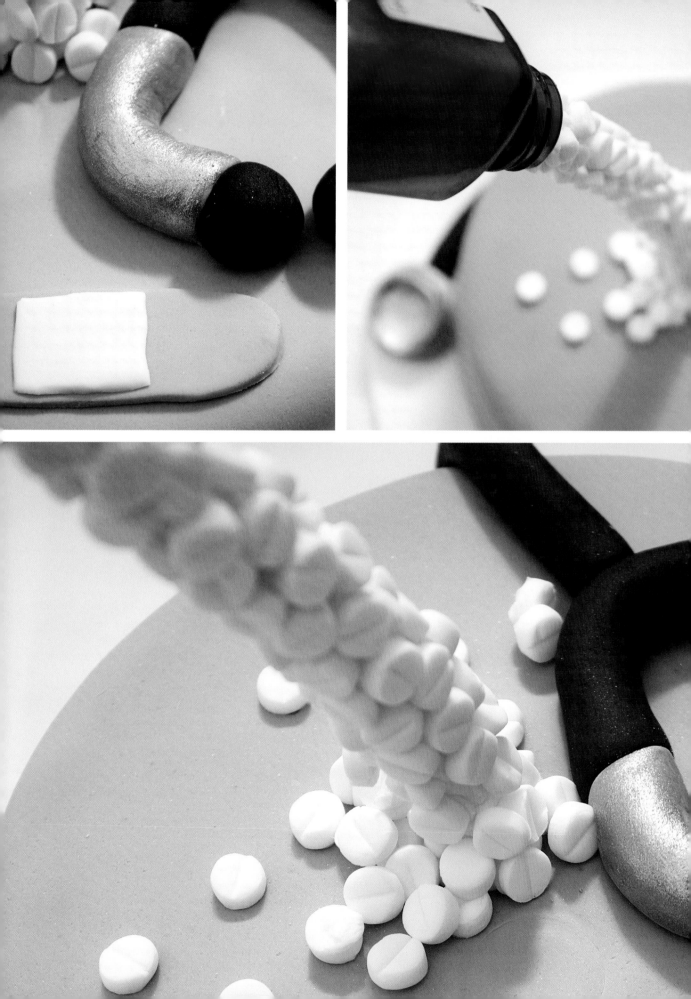

MOTHER'S DAY GIFT

The sweetest gift for the sweetest mother! What better way to show your mom how much you love her than to bake her this scrumptious jewelry box cake. Feeds 25.

GETTING STARTED

Melt the candy wafers, attach the balloon stick to the front right side of the round cake board, about 3 inches (7.5 cm) from the edge, and let set. Spread a small dollop of icing around the base of the stick. Center the first cake over the cake board and slide it down the stick. Cover the top with icing. Center and slide the second cake down the stick. Crumb-coat the entire cake. Set the third cake aside. Slide the 18-gauge wires down inside the stick and trim the stick and wires to the height of the jewelry bag plus about 7 inches (18 cm) from the top of the cake.

EQUIPMENT

- Balloon stick
- 12-inch (30 cm) round cake board
- Three 18-gauge wires
- Mini display jewelry bag
- Rolling pin
- Cake smoother
- 6-inch (15 cm) thin square cake board
- Four 6-inch (15 cm) cake pop sticks
- Small paintbrush
- 13 feet (4 m) lightweight display beads
- Small hair tie or elastic band
- Parchment paper

INGREDIENTS

- 1 tbsp (15 mL) candy coating wafers
- 2½ cups (625 mL) butter icing
- Three 6-inch (15 cm) square cakes, leveled
- 30 oz (850 g) turquoise fondant
- 25 oz (725 g) white fondant
- Small bowl of water
- 4½ tbsp (67 mL) royal icing mix

1 Using the rolling pin, roll out 20 oz (575 g) turquoise fondant into a sheet large enough to cover the entire two-layer cake (the jewelry box).

2 Slide the sheet down the balloon stick so it drapes over the cake. Use the cake smoother to smooth the top and sides of the cake. Trim off any excess fondant. Smooth again.

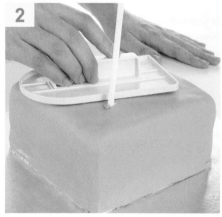

3 Spread a small dollop of icing over the square cake board and place the third cake (the lid) on top. Place the cake board on an upside-down bowl (see tip, page 208). Crumb-coat the cake.

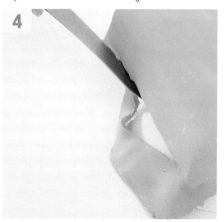

4 Using the rolling pin, roll out the remaining turquoise fondant until smooth and very thin. Drape the fondant over the third cake, smooth the top and sides and trim off any excess.

TIPS

If you want to add a second layer of icing to the cakes before applying the fondant, you will need an additional 2 cups (500 mL) icing for this recipe.

To prevent fondant from becoming sticky, dust your work surface with confectioners' (icing) sugar before working with it.

Placing the square cake board on top of an upside-down bowl (or a tall glass) makes it easier to drape the fondant over the cake and trim the sides.

You will be using a total of about 10 oz (300 g) to form the tissue paper pieces in steps 7 to 9.

In step 9, hold the lid over the two-layer cake, at the angle you want it to sit, to see exactly how much of the sides of the jewelry box you will need to cover in tissue paper.

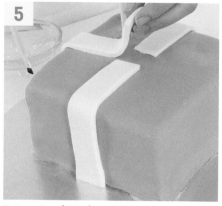

Roll out 7 oz (200 g) white fondant until smooth and very thin. Cut four 1-inch (2.5 cm) wide strips, about 2½ inches (6 cm) taller than the jewelry box. Using water as glue, attach one strip vertically to the center of each side, draping it over the top.

Cut four 1-inch (2.5 cm) wide strips long enough to reach from the center of the lid down the side. Using water as glue, attach one strip to each side of the cake, draping them over the top to meet in the center.

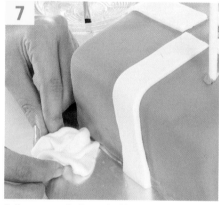

Roll out a small piece of white fondant into a smooth, very thin strip. Gently crimp the sides together, to resemble crumpled tissue paper. Using water as glue, attach the piece to the cake board, in front of the jewelry box.

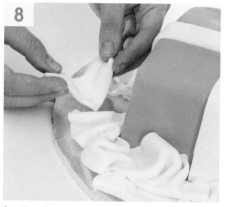

Continue forming tissue paper pieces (see tip) and attaching them to the cake board until the base of the jewelry box is hidden.

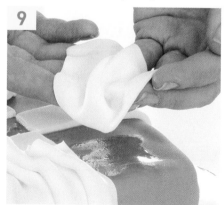

Form more tissue paper pieces and attach them to drape from the top over the front and side edges of the jewelry box, going only about halfway along each side edge (see tip).

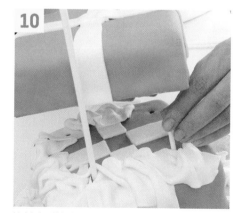

Hold the lid above where you want it to sit on the jewelry box (behind the tissue paper) and use a cake pop stick to mark 4 points on the cake that will lie under the lid and, when bolstered, will ensure even support for it.

Cut the cake pop sticks to the exact height of the jewelry box and slide a stick into the cake at each of the 4 marked points.

In a small bowl, combine 1½ tbsp (22 mL) royal icing mix and 1 tsp (5 mL) water. Using this mixture as glue, attach the lid to the top of the jewelry box.

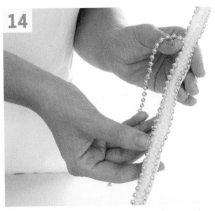

Starting at the top and working down, mold 1 oz (30 g) white fondant around the balloon stick. Bend the stick to a natural pouring angle.

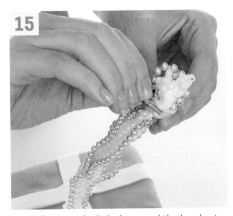

Using the paintbrush, brush the fondant on the stick with water. Gently press beads into the fondant all the way up the stick until the fondant is covered and the beads are secure.

Carefully wrap the hair tie around the beads at the top of the stick, locking them into place. Slide the jewelry bag down the stick. Loosely cover the cake with a kitchen towel and set in a cool spot.

For the bow, roll out half of the remaining white fondant until flat and smooth. Cut into strips about 3¼ inches (8 cm) long and ¾ inch (2 cm) wide. Repeat with the remaining white fondant. until you have 16 strips (see tips).

TIPS

Loosely covering the cake with a clean kitchen towel at the end of step 15 prevents dust from falling on it while you are preparing and drying the bow loops. Alternatively, you could prepare the loops the day before you start this project.

In step 16, be careful not to roll the fondant for the bow loops out too thin. You will only be using 13 loops for the bow, but cut 16 strips so you have enough extra to make up for any mistakes or imperfect loops.

When cutting strips, use a clean plastic ruler to help you cut straight lines.

TIP

If you don't have 24 hours to spare for the bow loops to set, add CMC (Tylose powder) to the fondant before you make the loops and they will dry in about 4 hours.

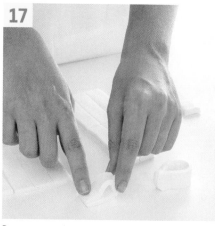

Dampen one side of each strip with water and fold the other side over to form a loop, pressing the ends together firmly.

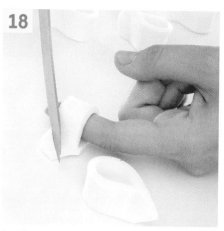

Cut the ends of each loop into a triangular point. Using your hands, fix any imperfections in the loops until they hold a smooth, even shape. Place on parchment paper and let set for at least 24 hours to dry completely (see tip).

In a small bowl, combine the remaining royal icing mix and 2 tsp (10 mL) water. Scoop a small circle into the center of the lid.

Arrange 6 loops in a circle around the edges of the icing mix, affixing the triangular ends in the mixture.

Add another dollop of icing mix to the center, covering the triangular ends. Affix another circle of loops, angled up rather than lying flat and staggered so that each loop lies between two loops below.

Add another small dollop of icing mix to the center and affix the final loop so that it is standing straight up.

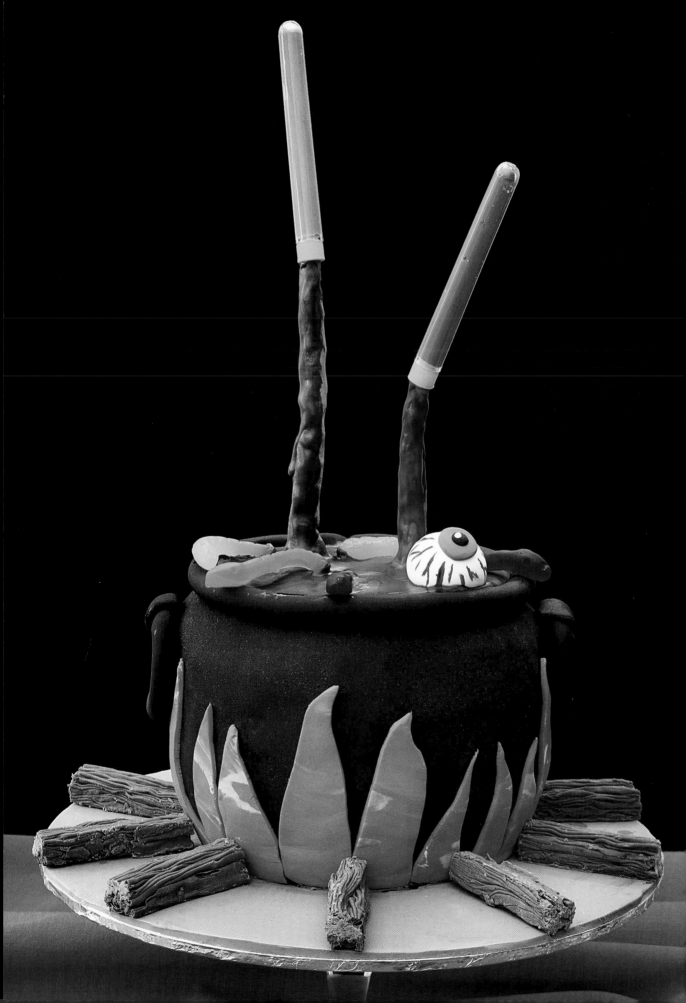

HALLOWEEN CAULDRON

Cast a spell on Halloween with this festive cauldron cake. Our easy decorating tips will help you create the spookiest cake to feed all your visiting ghouls! Feeds 30.

GETTING STARTED

Stack the 4 cakes, smothering icing between each layer. Using a serrated knife, carve a rounded edge around the top cake. Carve downward around the base cake to create a bowl shape. Crumb-coat the entire cake. Let stand for 1 hour or until thawed completely. Meanwhile, melt 2 tbsp (30 mL) candy wafers, attach the balloon sticks about 1 inch (2.5 cm) apart in the center of the cake board and let set. Spread a small dollop of icing around the base of each stick. Center the cake over the cake board and slide the cake down the sticks.

EQUIPMENT

- Serrated knife
- Two balloon sticks
- 12-inch (30 cm) round cake board
- Rolling pin
- Cake smoother
- Pastry brush
- ½-inch (1 cm) circle cutter
- Small, thin paintbrush
- Six 18-gauge wires
- 2 test tubes

INGREDIENTS

- Four 7-inch (18 cm) cakes, leveled and frozen
- 2½ cups (625 mL) butter icing
- 5 tbsp (75 mL) milk chocolate candy coating wafers
- 41 oz (1.2 kg) black fondant
- Small bowl of water
- 6 oz (175 g) red fondant
- 2 oz (60 g) yellow fondant
- 1 oz (30 g) white fondant

1 Using the rolling pin, roll out 35 oz (1 kg) black fondant into a sheet large enough to cover the entire cake. Slide the sheet down the balloon sticks so it drapes over the cake. Smooth the fondant and trim off any excess. Smooth again.

2 Using your hands, roll 4 oz (125 g) black fondant into a tube long enough to wrap around the cake (about 22 inches/55 cm long).

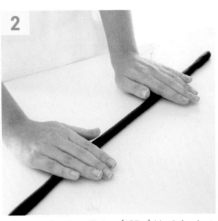

3 Using water as glue, attach the tube to the top of the cake, around the perimeter. Trim off any excess fondant and press the ends of the tube together. Set excess fondant aside.

4 Roll 1 oz (30 g) black fondant into a 5-inch (12.5 cm) long tube. Cut a sliver off each end of the tube to flatten it. Using water as glue, stick the ends together, forming a circle. Repeat with another 1 oz black fondant.

continued on next page

INGREDIENTS

- 1¼ oz (38 g) green fondant
- Red gel food coloring
- 1½ oz (45 g) purple fondant
- 6 tbsp (90 mL) royal icing mix
- Purple gel food coloring
- Green gel food coloring
- Gummy worms
- 4 oz (125 g) long, flaky chocolate sticks

TIPS

To prevent fondant from becoming sticky, dust your work surface with confectioners' (icing) sugar before working with it.

If desired, after step 1 cover the cake board with 10 oz (300 g) purple fondant (see page 33).

In step 7, use a knife to gently press the bottom of each flame down around the base of the cauldron until it is firmly attached.

Press the slivers of black fondant into 2 flat strips. Wrap a strip around the seam on each circle. Using water as glue, attach the handles on either side of the cake, near the top.

Lightly knead together the red and yellow fondant until a swirled effect forms. Roll out the fondant into a wide strip and cut out flame shapes.

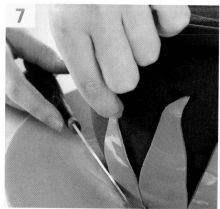

Using the pastry brush, dampen the lower half of the cake with water and attach the flames all the way around (see tip).

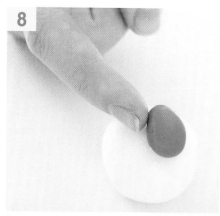

For the eyeball, set aside a pinch of white fondant and roll the rest into a ball. Roll out ⅛ oz (4 g) green fondant and cut out a circle with the circle cutter. Using water as glue, attach the circle to the ball.

Form a pinch of excess black fondant into a small circle and attach it in the center of the green circle, as the pupil. Form the reserved pinch of white fondant into a tiny circle and attach it near one edge of the pupil.

Dip the paintbrush in red food coloring and paint wiggly veins on the eyeball. Set aside.

11

Slide 3 wires inside each balloon stick. Trim one stick and its wires to the height of a test tube plus 5 inches (12.5 cm) from the top of the cake. Trim the other stick and its wires to the height of a test tube plus 3 inches (7.5 cm).

12

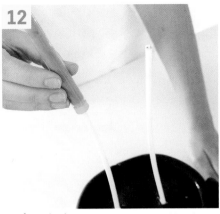

Roll ¼ oz (8 g) purple fondant into a thin tube and push it inside a test tube. Slide the test tube down the longer stick. Mold the remaining purple fondant around the rest of the stick.

13

Repeat step 12 on the other stick with the remaining green fondant and the other test tube. Bend the sticks away from each other to a natural pouring angle.

14

In a small bowl, combine 3 tbsp (45 mL) royal icing mix, 1 tsp (5 mL) water and 1 drop purple food coloring. Spoon over the half of the cake under the purple stick and brush it up over the stick.

15

Repeat step 14 in a separate bowl with green food coloring, spooning the mixture over the other half of the cake and brushing it up over the stick. Use a knife to swirl and blur the line between the mixtures.

16

Arrange the gummy worms and eyeball on the cake. Melt the remaining candy wafers. Trim the chocolate sticks as needed. Using the melted chocolate as glue, place the sticks on the cake board around the cake, as fire logs.

TIPS

In steps 14 and 15, the mixtures should be a liquid consistency; if they are a little dry, add a bit more water. You can also add more food coloring as necessary to reach your desired color.

If you want to add a second layer of icing to the cake before applying the fondant, you will need an additional 2½ cups (625 mL) icing for this recipe.

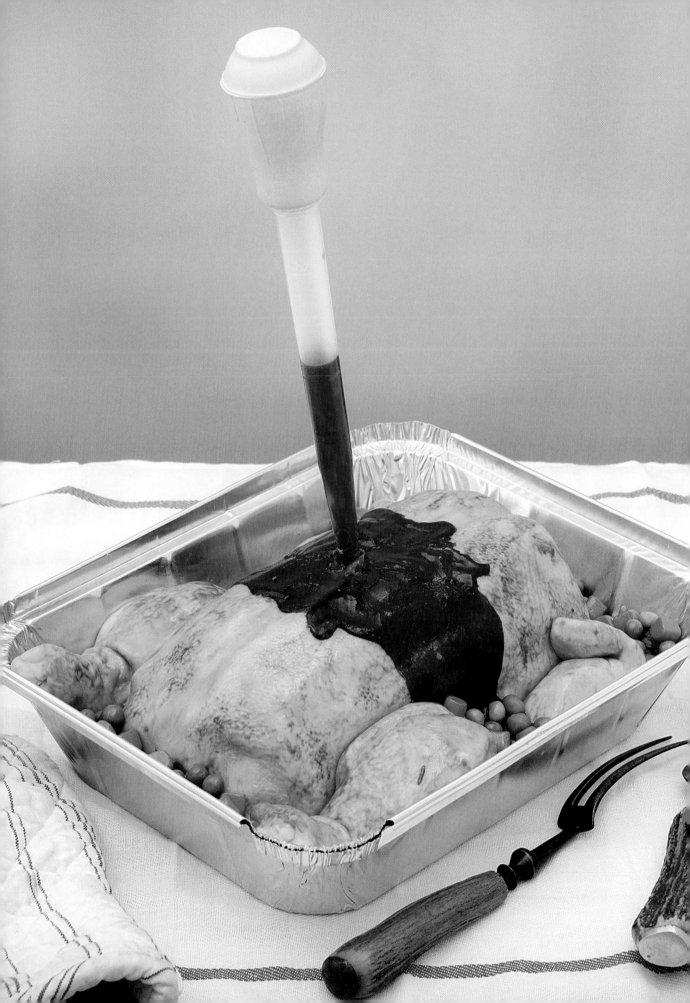

TURKEY DINNER

GETTING STARTED

Melt 1 tbsp (15 mL) candy wafers, attach the balloon stick to the center of the baking pan and let set.

Using the serrated knife, cut the frozen cakes in half vertically, creating 4 rectangles. Set one of the halves aside to thaw. Stack the other 3 cakes, smothering icing between each layer.

Carve downward around the border of the stacked cake to create a rounded rectangular shape. (This will form the body of your turkey, so don't make it too thin or flat.)

Crumb-coat the cake, loosely cover it with a clean kitchen towel and set it aside to thaw completely, about 1 hour.

When the cake is thawed, spread a dollop of icing around the base of the balloon stick, center the cake over the stick and slide it down the stick.

Surprise your family this Thanksgiving by serving a giant turkey, with a side of peas and carrots, to gobble up for dessert! This amazingly realistic design will wow all your dinner guests into thinking it's the real thing. An enormous cake to feed the whole family, and then some. Feeds 35.

EQUIPMENT

- Balloon stick
- 13- by 10-inch (33 by 25 cm) foil baking pan (see tip, page 220)
- Serrated knife
- Rolling pin
- Texture fondant impression mat
- Baking sheet lined with parchment paper
- Pastry brush
- Three 18-gauge wires
- Plastic baster with a hole wider than the balloon stick
- Small paintbrush

INGREDIENTS

- 2 tbsp (30 mL) milk chocolate candy coating wafers
- Two 10-inch (25 cm) square cakes, frozen

continued on next page

INGREDIENTS

- 3¾ cups (925 mL) butter icing
- 35 oz (1 kg) cream fondant
- Small bowl of water
- Brown gel food coloring
- 3½ oz (100 g) green fondant
- 3½ oz (100 g) orange fondant
- ½ cup (125 mL) royal icing mix
- 2 tbsp (30 mL) confectioners' glaze

TIPS

Using a foil baking pan is optional; if you prefer, you can use a cake board instead. If using a foil pan, make sure it is strong enough to hold the cake. If you can't find one strong enough, stack two pans, melting some chocolate onto the base pan to act as glue.

To ensure that your mixture is the right consistency in step 9, roll a small piece into a ball in your palm. If the mixture does not crumble, it is ready to go! Add more icing if it crumbles.

Using the rolling pin, roll out 27 oz (775 g) cream fondant into a sheet large enough to cover the entire cake. Stamp the fondant with the fondant impression mat.

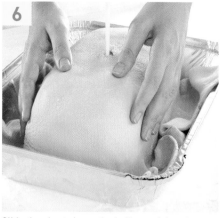

Slide the sheet down the balloon stick so it drapes over the cake. Using your fingers, gently mold the fondant onto the cake. Trim off any excess fondant.

Using your index finger, gently press an indented line lengthwise across the top of the cake, along the center line. Loosely cover the cake with a kitchen towel and set in a cool spot.

Slice the reserved cake half through the middle to make sure it is completely thawed. Place both halves in a large bowl and crumble into fine crumbs (or use an electric mixer to beat to fine crumbs).

Gradually add icing, 1 tbsp (15 mL) at a time, mixing it with the cake crumbs until the mixture is the consistency of a soft dough (see tip).

Set about one-quarter of the cake mixture aside. Divide the remaining cake mixture in half and form each half into the shape of a turkey drumstick.

11

Divide the reserved cake mixture in half and form each half into the shape of a turkey wing. Place the wings and drumsticks on the prepared baking sheet and refrigerate for at least 3 hours, until the mixture hardens and holds its shape.

12

Smother the chilled drumstick and wing shapes in icing.

13

Using the rolling pin, roll out the remaining cream fondant until thin and smooth. Cut out 4 squares large enough to wrap each drumstick and wing. Wrap fondant around each drumstick and wing, molding the seams together (see tip).

14

Using water as glue, gently attach the drumsticks and wings to the side of the cake, using the photo as a guide for positioning and placement.

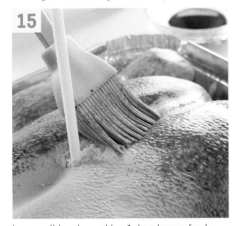

15

In a small bowl, combine 1 drop brown food coloring and 2 tsp (10 mL) water. Using the pastry brush, dab food coloring all over the turkey.

16

Form the green fondant into balls the size of peas. Form the orange fondant into pieces the size of small carrot chunks, pressing on the sides to give the pieces a more squared shape.

TIPS

To prevent fondant from becoming sticky, dust your work surface with confectioners' (icing) sugar before working with it.

Loosely covering the cake with a clean kitchen towel at the end of step 7 prevents dust from falling on it while you are preparing and chilling the drumsticks and wings. Alternatively, you could prepare the drumsticks and wings the night before you start this project.

Don't worry about perfecting the seams in step 13 — just place the smoother side face out in step 14. Gently reshape the pieces if they lose shape during the wrapping process.

In step 18, you are trying to create a mixture with a stiff liquid consistency; it shouldn't be too runny. Tweak the mixture with more royal icing mixture or water as needed.

If you want to add a second layer of icing to the cake before applying the fondant, you will need an additional 3 cups (750 mL) icing for this recipe.

Arrange the peas and carrots around the cake, covering the base of the pan.

In a small bowl, combine royal icing mix, 2 drops brown food coloring and 2 tbsp (30 mL) water. Drizzle over the turkey, around the balloon stick, then use a spoon to guide the mixture down the sides.

Let the cake set for about 1 hour, then, using the pastry brush, brush the entire cake, including veggies, with confectioners' glaze.

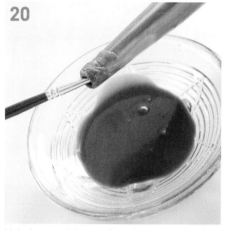

Melt the remaining candy wafers and, using the paintbrush, paint inside the bottom of the baster with melted candy, being careful not to block the hole. Let dry, then paint a second coat.

Slide the 18-gauge wires down inside the balloon stick and trim the stick and wires to the height of the baster.

Once the melted candy is completely set, slide the baster down the balloon stick.

SANTA CLAUS

Spread the festive spirit with this amazing Santa Claus cake! You'll stay off the naughty list when you bring this four-layer cake to your Christmas party. Feeds 25.

GETTING STARTED

Melt the candy wafers, attach the balloon stick to the center of the cake board and let set. Spread a small dollop of icing around the base of the stick. Center the first cake over the stick and slide it down the stick. Cover the top with icing. Repeat with the second and third cakes. Center and slide the fourth cake down the stick. Crumb-coat the entire cake. Fill the pastry bag with the remaining icing. Slide the 18-gauge wires down inside the stick and trim the stick and wires to the height of the red sack plus about 2 inches (5 cm) from the top of the cake.

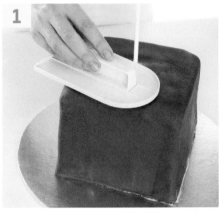

Using the rolling pin, roll out the brown fondant into a sheet large enough to cover the cake. Slide the sheet down the balloon stick so it drapes over the cake. Smooth the cake and trim off excess fondant. Smooth again.

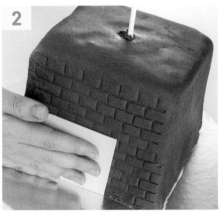

Press the fondant on the sides of the cake with the brick impression mat, so it looks like a chimney.

In a small bowl, combine 3 drops brown food coloring and 2 tbsp (30 mL) water (see tip, page 226). Using the paintbrush, brush the food coloring over the chimney to highlight the brick texture.

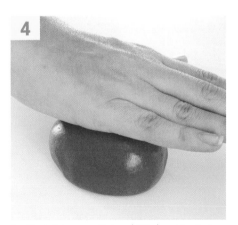

For Santa's torso, roll 4 oz (125 g) red fondant into a ball, then gently press the ball against a flat surface, creating a flattened oval wide enough to hold Santa's legs.

EQUIPMENT

- Balloon stick
- 12-inch (30 cm) round cake board
- Pastry bag fitted with a #804 or #2A (1 cm) round tip
- Three 18-gauge wires
- Small red display sack
- Rolling pin
- Cake smoother
- Brick-texture fondant impression mat
- Small paintbrush
- 6-inch (15 cm) cake pop stick, cut in half
- Bow fondant mold
- 8 inches (20 cm) black string
- Small fine-mesh sieve

INGREDIENTS

- 1 tbsp (15 mL) candy coating wafers
- 6 cups (1.5 L) vanilla butter icing (see tip, page 226)
- Four 6-inch (15 cm) square cakes, leveled
- 30 oz (850 g) brown fondant
- Brown gel food coloring

continued on next page

INGREDIENTS

- 13 oz (400 g) red fondant
- Small bowl of water
- 2½ oz (75 g) white fondant
- 1 oz (30 g) black fondant
- Gold edible paint
- 6 oz (175 g) blue fondant
- 6 oz (175 g) green fondant
- 1 cup (250 mL) confectioners' (icing) sugar

TIPS

Try using colorless vanilla extract to ensure that your icing is extra-white. This will help make it look more realistic as snow.

If you want to add a second layer of icing to the cake before applying the fondant, you will need an additional 3 cups (750 mL) icing for this recipe.

Before brushing the chimney in step 3, press a spare piece of brown fondant with the brick impression mat and brush it with the food coloring mixture to make sure it is the desired color. Add more food coloring or water to the mixture if desired.

5 Dampen the ends of the cake pop stick halves with water and slide them into the torso where the legs will sit.

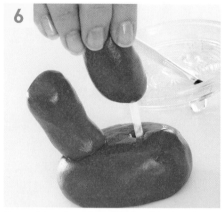

6 For each leg, form 1 oz (30 g) red fondant into a thick, stumpy cylinder. Dampen the torso around the sticks and slide each leg down a stick. Using your fingers, blend the seams between torso and legs.

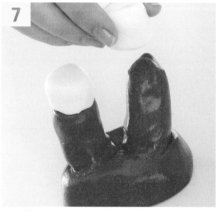

7 Form ½ oz (15 g) white fondant into 2 thick flattened circles the same diameter as the legs. Using water as glue, attach a circle to the end of each leg, for Santa's pant cuffs.

8 For the shoes, form ½ oz (15 g) black fondant into 2 thick ovals. Using a knife, carefully slice an indent in each sole to define the heel, wiggling the knife gently to make a wider gap.

9 Using water as glue, attach the shoes, sole side up, to the top of the pant cuffs.

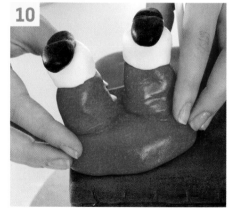

10 Dampen the surface of the cake and attach Santa's torso, legs up, in front and to the left of the balloon stick.

11

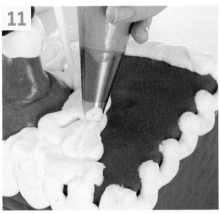

Pipe a scalloped border around the top of the chimney. Fill in the exposed surface on top of the cake with icing, gently smoothing it with a knife. Use any remaining icing to add height to the snow (see tip).

12

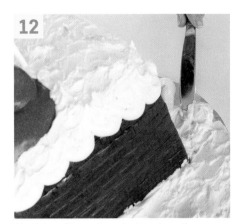

Pipe icing all over the cake board, gently smoothing it with a knife to form a snow pile that gets thicker as it reaches the cake.

13

For the hat, form 1 oz (30 g) red fondant into a thick, tall triangle. Bend the tip of the hat. Roll a small piece of white fondant into a ball and, using water as glue, attach it to the tip of the hat.

14

Form a pinch of white fondant into a thin strip that fits across the base of the hat. Using water as glue, attach the strip to the base of the hat. Nestle the hat into the snow on the cake board, at the front.

15

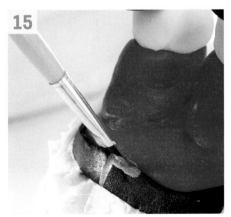

Form ½ oz (15 g) black fondant into a thin strip long enough to wrap around Santa's belly. Using water as glue, wrap it around his belly. Using gold paint, paint a small buckle at the front of the belt.

16

For the gifts, form two 2-oz (60 g) red fondant cubes, two 1-oz (30 g) red cubes, two 2-oz blue cubes, two 1-oz blue cubes, two 2-oz green cubes and two 1-oz green cubes, gently pressing the side of each cube against a flat surface.

To prevent fondant from becoming sticky, dust your work surface with confectioners' (icing) sugar before working with it.

In step 11, be sure not to add too much height to the snow around Santa's torso, as you need room to add his belt.

When cutting strips, use a clean plastic ruler to help you cut straight lines.

In step 17, 12 of the strips should be long enough to run across 3 sides of a large cube, and 12 should be long enough to cross 3 sides of a small cube.

You may need to trim the balloon stick a little more once you've placed your gifts around the stick in step 21. Slide the sack down the string to check; there shouldn't be any gap between the gifts and the sack.

If desired, in step 22 stuff the sack with cotton balls before sliding it down the stick, so it looks pleasantly plump.

Using the rolling pin, roll out the remaining white fondant until thin and smooth. Cut into 24 strips about ⅛ inch (3 mm) wide (see tip).

Dip the paintbrush in water and brush a line that runs through the center across 3 sides of a cube. Wrap a strip over the dampened line, smoothing it and trimming off the edges.

Using a brushed line of water as glue, attach another strip perpendicular to the first strip, crossing the first strip at the top of the cube and running down the uncovered sides. Repeat steps 18 and 19 for all of the cubes.

Using the bow mold, create 12 small white fondant bows. Using water as glue, attach a bow at the top of each cube, where the strips cross.

Nestle 3 large gifts in the snow around the base of the balloon stick, then arrange the remaining gifts as desired on the cake and cake board (see tip), nestling them in the icing.

Slide the sack down the stick and tie it closed with black string, securing it to the stick. Using the sieve, dust the cake with sugar to give the snow a fluffy, powdery finish.

DEEP-DISH PIZZA

Take your pizza cravings to new heights with this deep-dish pie smothered with fondant olives. Feeds 20.

GETTING STARTED

Spread some icing over the 12-inch (30 cm) cake board where the cake will sit, to prevent it from sliding. Place the first cake in the center of the board and cover the top with icing. Place the second cake on top.

Cut out a wedge from the cake that is about one-eighth of it (see tip, page 232). Place the wedge on the thin cake board and trace around it carefully with a knife. Cut out the shape from the cake board.

Crumb-coat the entire cake, including the inside of the cutout.

Cover the board wedge in icing and place the cake wedge on top. Crumb-coat the cake wedge and set it aside.

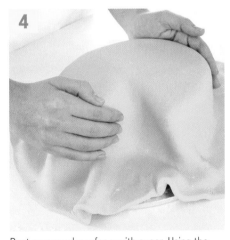

Dust your work surface with sugar. Using the rolling pin, roll out 24 oz (700 g) cream fondant into a sheet large enough to cover the entire cake. Drape the sheet over the cake and use your fingers to mold it into the cutout.

EQUIPMENT

- 12-inch (30 cm) round cake board
- Thin cake board (any size)
- Rolling pin
- Cake smoother
- Lightweight pizza slice server
- 3½-inch (9 cm) tall slim transparent shot glass
- Pastry brush
- ⅝-inch (1.5 cm) circle cutter
- Parchment paper
- Box grater

INGREDIENTS

- 2½ cups (625 mL) butter icing
- Two 8-inch (20 cm) round cakes, leveled and frozen
- Confectioners' (icing) sugar
- 42 oz (1.2 kg) cream fondant
- ⅔ cup (150 mL) royal icing mix
- Small bowl of water
- 1 oz (30 g) black fondant
- Brown gel food coloring

continued on next page

INGREDIENTS

- Red gel food coloring
- 5 oz (150 g) pale cream fondant, frozen
- 6 oz (175 g) pale cream fondant

TIP

In step 1, gently score lines where you plan to cut out the wedge before actually cutting it, to make sure you are happy with the size.

Use the cake smoother to smooth the top and sides of the cake. Trim off any excess fondant. Smooth again.

Roll out 10 oz (300 g) cream fondant into a sheet large enough to cover the wedge. Place the wedge on a tall glass and drape the sheet over top. Smooth the fondant and trim off any excess.

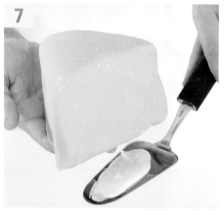

In a small bowl, combine 1½ tbsp (22 mL) royal icing mix and 1 tsp (5 mL) water. Set aside 1 tsp (5 mL) of the mixture and spoon the rest onto the pizza server. Place the wedge on the server.

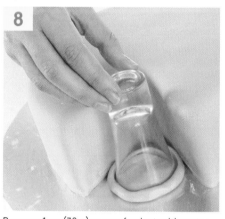

Dampen 1 oz (30 g) cream fondant with water and press it onto the cake board where the wedge is cut out. Gently press the shot glass, rim down, into the fondant.

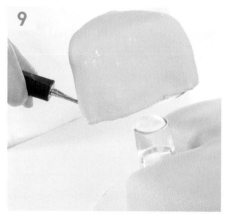

Coat the top of the shot glass with the remaining icing mixture and place the server on top, as if you have just pulled out the wedge, holding it in place until it is secure.

Roll the remaining cream fondant into a tube long enough to wrap around the entire cake if there was no cutout (about 25 inches/63 cm long). Cut off a piece the length of the rounded side of the wedge.

11

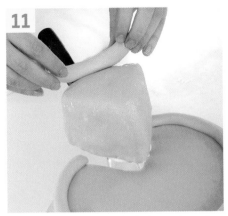

Using water as glue, attach the long tube to the top of the cake, around the perimeter, starting and ending at the cutout. Attach the short tube to the top of the wedge.

12

For the olives, roll out the black fondant into a thick sheet. Using the circle cutter, cut out circles. Using the tip of a small paintbrush (see tip), stamp a hole in the center of each. Place on the parchment paper and let set.

13

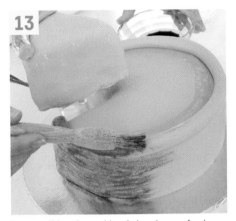

In a small bowl, combine 1 drop brown food coloring and 1 tbsp (15 mL) water. Using the pastry brush, paint the sides of the cake and the tubes with the food coloring (see tip).

14

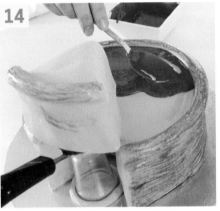

In another bowl, combine the remaining royal icing mix, 4 drops red food coloring, 1 drop brown food coloring and 2 tbsp (30 mL) water (see tip). Spread most of this mixture over the top of the cake and the wedge.

15

Using the large holes of the box grater, grate the frozen pale cream fondant into a bowl. Set aside a pinch of grated fondant and sprinkle the remainder over the top of the cake and the wedge.

16

Scatter all but 4 of the olives over the cake and wedge, pressing them gently into the red mixture to secure them.

TIPS

In step 12, any thin, round tool can be used to stamp the holes in the center of the olives. After stamping them, let the olives set on the parchment paper until you are ready to use them.

Before painting the crust in step 13, brush some of the food coloring onto a small scrap of cream fondant to test the color. Add more food coloring or water as necessary.

In step 14, you are trying to create a mixture with a stiff liquid consistency; it shouldn't be too runny. Tweak the mixture with more royal icing mixture or water as needed.

If you want to add a second layer of icing to the cake before applying the fondant, you will need an additional 1¼ cups (300 mL) icing for this recipe.

If your fondant starts to get sticky, keep dusting your work surface with confectioners' (icing) sugar.

17

Roll out the 6 oz (175 g) pale cream fondant into a thin sheet. Cut into strips, some long enough to hang from the top of the wedge to the cake, and some long enough to hang to the cake board.

18

Dampen the sides of the wedge with water and attach the shorter strips, draping them slightly over the top of the wedge and letting them hang down to the cake. Attach the longer strips just below the tube at the back of the wedge, letting them hang down to the cake board.

19

Coat the seams of the strips on top of the cake with some of the remaining red mixture. Sprinkle the reserved pinch of grated fondant on top.

20

Using the remaining red mixture as glue, attach the remaining olives here and there on the strips.

> Stuffed with your favorite cake, this dessert pizza is oozing with delicious surprises.

SUSHI SELECTION

GETTING STARTED

Melt the candy wafers, attach the balloon stick to the right-hand side of the cake board, about 3 inches (7.5 cm) from the edge, and let set. Spread a bit of icing over the cake board where the cake will sit. Center the cake above the cake board and slide it down the stick. Crumb-coat the cake. Slide the 18-gauge wires down inside the stick and trim the stick and wires to the height of the soy sauce bottle plus about 4 inches (10 cm) from the top of the cake.

Dust your work surface with sugar. Using the rolling pin, roll out the dark brown fondant into a sheet large enough to cover the entire cake. Press the fondant with the wood-grain impression mat.

Slide the sheet down the balloon stick so it drapes over the cake. Use the cake smoother to smooth the top and sides of the cake. Trim off any excess fondant. Smooth again and reapply texture if needed.

Practice your fondant skills to design amazing-looking sushi pieces, complete with wasabi and ginger!

EQUIPMENT

- Balloon stick
- 12-inch (30 cm) square cake board
- Three 18-gauge wires
- Mini display soy sauce bottle
- Rolling pin
- Wood-grain fondant impression mat
- Cake smoother
- Small paintbrush
- Parchment paper
- Chopsticks

INGREDIENTS

- 1 tbsp (15 mL) candy coating wafers
- 1 cup (250 mL) butter icing
- One 8-inch (20 cm) square cake, leveled
- Confectioners' (icing) sugar
- 18 oz (525 g) dark brown fondant
- 11¼ oz (340 g) white fondant
- 4 oz (125 g) dark green fondant (see tip, page 238)
- Small bowl of water
- 1⅛ oz (35 g) light green fondant
- 1⅜ oz (40 g) orange fondant
- ½ oz (15 g) black fondant
- 1 tbsp (15 mL) royal icing mix
- Black gel food coloring

TIPS

If you can't find green fondant that is the right color for seaweed (nori), try mixing a little black fondant in with dark green fondant.

If you want to add a second layer of icing to the cake before applying the fondant, you will need an additional ⅔ cup (150 mL) icing for this recipe.

3 Divide 5 oz (150 g) white fondant into 5 equal pieces. Using the palms of your hands, roll each piece into a thick cylinder.

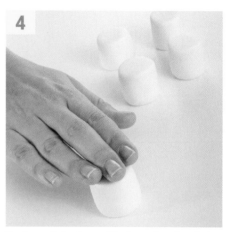

4 Gently push the top and bottom of each cylinder against your work surface to flatten the edges.

5 Using the rolling pin, roll out the dark green fondant until thin and smooth. Cut out 5 small, neat rectangles, each slightly wider than the height of a cylinder and long enough to wrap around it.

6 Using the paintbrush, brush one side of a rectangle with water. Place a cylinder on its side, with the bottom touching one long edge of the rectangle, and roll the rectangle around the cylinder, trimming off any excess.

7 Press the seam on the sushi roll to seal it, then gently roll the piece between the palms of your hands to secure it. Repeat steps 6 and 7 to create 5 sushi rolls.

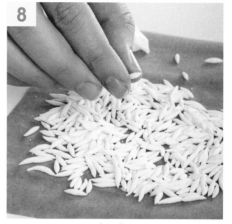

8 Using a total of 1 oz (30 g) white fondant, pinch off tiny pieces and roll them gently between your thumb and finger to create grains of rice. Place rice on parchment paper.

9

Using ⅛ oz (4 g) light green fondant and ⅛ oz (4 g) orange fondant, form 3 green and 2 orange circles that will fit in the center of the sushi rolls with room around them for rice.

10

Brush the top of each sushi roll with water and place a green or orange circle in the center. Sprinkle rice around the circles.

TIPS

If your fondant starts to get sticky, keep dusting your work surface with confectioners' (icing) sugar.

If desired, after step 2 cover the cake board with 10 oz (300 g) light brown fondant (see page 33) and press it all the way around with the wood-grain impression mat.

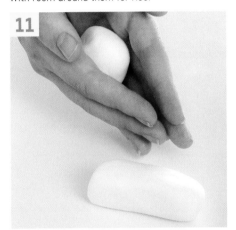

11

Divide 3 oz (90 g) white fondant in half and form into 2 long, rounded rectangles (the bases for nigiri).

12

Use the rolling pin to gently blend together ¼ oz (8 g) orange fondant and ¼ oz (8 g) white fondant until white streaks are running through the orange, resembling salmon. Form into 2 long, rounded rectangles.

13

Brush the tops of the white nigiri bases with water and top each with a salmon piece. Stick rice all over the sides of each white base.

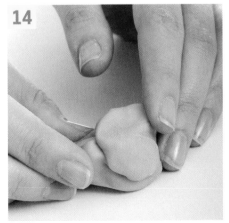

14

For wasabi, form 1 oz (30 g) light green fondant into a loose pile.

TIP

In step 20, you are trying to create a mixture with a stiff liquid consistency; it shouldn't be too runny. Tweak the mixture with more royal icing mixture or water as needed.

15

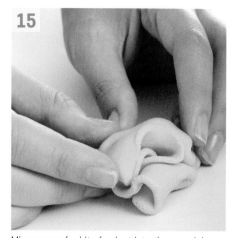

Mix scraps of white fondant into the remaining orange fondant to make it paler. Using the rolling pin, roll it out until thin and smooth, then gently scrunch it to resemble a pile of ginger.

16

Use your hands to roll the remaining white fondant into a ball. Flatten the ball and push your thumb into the center to create a groove, then widen the groove to form a shallow bowl.

17

Center the bowl above the balloon stick and slide it down the stick. Use your fingers to touch up the bowl as necessary so it is smooth and even.

18

Using water as glue, arrange the sushi rolls, nigiri, wasabi, ginger and chopsticks on the cake.

19

Working from the top down, mold the black fondant around the portion of the balloon stick that will not be covered by the soy sauce bottle. Bend the stick to a natural pouring angle.

20

In a small bowl, combine royal icing mix, 3 drops black food coloring and 1 tsp (5 mL) water. Pour into the bowl and brush up over the fondant on the stick. Slide the soy sauce bottle down the stick.

WINE AND CHEESE

Add a chic centerpiece to a friendly get-together by creating this classic, elegant design. Sure to impress wine and cheese lovers everywhere! Feeds 20.

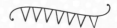

GETTING STARTED

Melt the candy wafers, attach the balloon stick to the center of the cake board and let set. Spread a small dollop of icing around the base of the stick. Center the first cake over the stick and slide it down the stick. Cover the top with icing. Center and slide the second cake down the stick. Crumb-coat the entire cake. Slide the 18-gauge wires down inside the stick and trim the stick and wires to the height of the wine bottle plus about 7 inches (18 cm) from the top of the cake.

EQUIPMENT

- Balloon stick
- 12-inch (30 cm) round cake board
- Three 18-gauge wires
- Small plastic display wine bottle
- Rolling pin
- Plastic wineglass with detachable base
- Small screwdriver or sharp tool
- Grape leaf cutter
- Small paintbrush

INGREDIENTS

- 1 tbsp (15 mL) candy coating wafers
- 2 cups (500 mL) butter icing
- Two 8-inch (20 cm) round cakes, leveled
- Confectioners' (icing) sugar
- 25 oz (725 g) white fondant
- 3 tbsp (45 mL) royal icing mix
- 7 oz (200 g) deep red fondant

Dust your work surface with sugar. Using the rolling pin, roll out 24 oz (700 g) white fondant into a sheet large enough to cover the entire cake.

Slide the sheet down the balloon stick so it drapes over the cake, allowing the sides to fall naturally, like the creases of a tablecloth. Trim off any excess fondant.

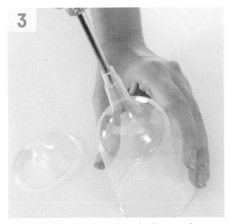

Separate the wineglass from its base and, using the screwdriver, carefully force a hole through the center of the base and through the stem of the glass (see tip, page 244). Reassemble the glass.

In a small bowl, combine royal icing mix and 2 tsp (10 mL) water. Dab this mixture on the bottom of the wineglass and slide the glass down the balloon stick, lightly pushing it down onto the cake.

continued on next page

INGREDIENTS

- 1 oz (30 g) brown fondant
- 2 oz (60 g) green fondant
- Small bowl of water
- 4 oz (125 g) purple fondant
- 1½ oz (45 g) bright red fondant
- 5½ oz (165 g) yellow fondant

TIPS

If you want to add a second layer of icing to the cake before applying the fondant, you will need an additional 1¼ cups (300 mL) icing for this recipe.

In step 3, the holes through the base and the stem need to be wide enough that you can slide the glass down the balloon stick, so make sure to use a tool of the appropriate size.

Drizzle some water inside the wineglass. Mound up 5 oz (150 g) deep red fondant and slide it down the stick into the glass. Gently mold the fondant to sit neatly in the glass.

Working from the top down, mold the remaining deep red fondant around the portion of the balloon stick that will not be covered by the wine bottle.

Roll a small piece of brown fondant into a thin stem. Using the rolling pin, roll out ¼ oz (8 g) green fondant until thin and smooth and use the leaf cutter to cut out 2 leaves.

Using water as glue, attach the leaves and stem to the top of the cake.

Roll small pieces of purple fondant into about 20 grape shapes. Using water as glue, attach a layer of grapes in a bunch shape below the leaves.

Using the paintbrush, brush the tops of the grapes with water and attach the remaining grapes on top, to create height.

Form 1 oz (30 g) bright red fondant into a thick disc. Cut out a small triangular wedge.

Roll out ¼ oz (8 g) yellow fondant and cut it into a rounded rectangle that, when folded at an angle, will fit inside the wedge cutout. Using water as glue, attach the rectangle to the inside of the cutout. Set aside.

TIP

If your fondant starts to get sticky, keep dusting your work surface with confectioners' (icing) sugar.

Form 4 oz (125 g) yellow fondant into a triangular cheese wedge. Gently push the bottom of the wedge against your work surface to flatten it.

Using ¼ oz (8 g) green fondant, roll ½-inch (1 cm) pieces, one at a time, between two fingers.

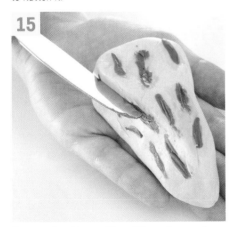

Dampen the sides and top of the yellow wedge with water. Squash the green pieces into the sides and top until they blend in. Drag a small knife across the green pieces, encouraging them to blend naturally.

Roll out the remaining brown fondant until flat and smooth. Cut out a piece that will fit neatly over the back of the cheese wedge. Using water as glue, attach the piece to the back of the cheese. Set aside.

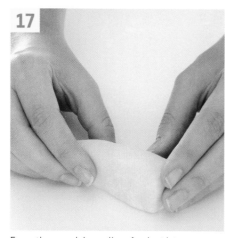

17

Form the remaining yellow fondant into a triangular cheese wedge.

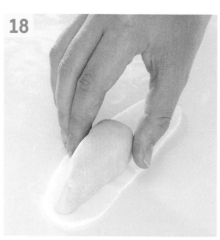

18

Roll out the remaining white fondant into a strip long and wide enough to wrap the yellow wedge lengthwise. Dampen the white fondant and place the wedge, resting on a long end, on top.

19

Wrap the white fondant over the wedge and gently blend the ends together. Slice along the sides to create a neat finish.

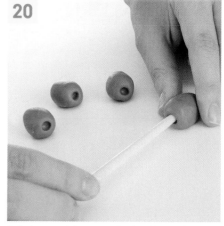

20

Roll the remaining green fondant into 4 olive shapes. Poke a small divot in the end of each olive.

21

Roll the remaining bright red fondant into 4 small balls and insert a ball into each olive divot.

22

Using water as glue, attach the cheese and olives to the cake (see tip). Slide the wine bottle down the balloon stick.

ROSE GARDEN

If you know a gardening fanatic, or you just fancy wowing your friends with your handiwork, this is the cake for you! Feeds 20.

GETTING STARTED

Melt the candy wafers, attach the balloon stick to the center of the cake board and let set. Spread a small dollop of uncolored icing around the base of the stick. Center the first cake over the stick and slide it down the stick. Cover the top with the uncolored icing. Center and slide the second cake down the stick. Crumb-coat the entire cake with the uncolored icing. Slide the 18-gauge wires down inside the stick and trim the stick and wires to the height of the watering can plus about 5 inches (12.5 cm) from the top of the cake.

EQUIPMENT

- Balloon stick
- 12-inch (30 cm) round cake board
- Three 18-gauge wires
- Lightweight mini watering can (see tip, page 250)
- Rolling pin
- Wood-grain fondant impression mat
- Small paintbrush
- Pastry bag fitted with a #233 grass tip

INGREDIENTS

- 1 tbsp (15 mL) candy coating wafers
- 2 cups (500 mL) butter icing
- Two 8-inch (20 cm) round cakes, leveled
- 22 oz (625 g) brown fondant
- 3 oz (90 g) gray fondant
- Small bowl of water
- Silver edible paint
- ½ cup (125 mL) butter icing, tinted green
- 16 dark chocolate cookies (about 7 oz/200 g)
- 2 oz (60 g) blue fondant
- 15 oz (450 g) pink fondant

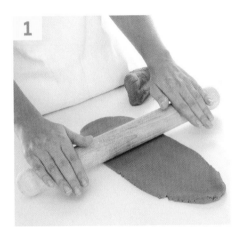

1 Using the rolling pin, roll out half the brown fondant into a thick strip about 13 inches (33 cm) long. Measure the height of the cake and add ½ inch (1 cm); trim the fondant to that height.

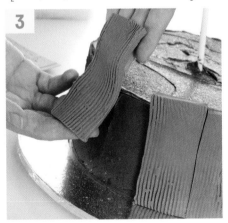

2 Press the fondant with the wood-grain impression mat and cut crosswise into thick strips about 1½ inches (4 cm) wide. Repeat steps 1 and 2 with the remaining brown fondant.

3 Place the strips vertically around the sides of the cake, one right next to the other, pressing them into the icing to adhere.

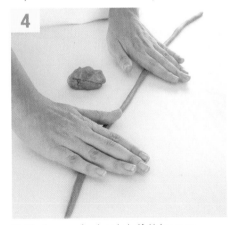

4 Divide the gray fondant in half. Using your hands, roll each half into a tube about 20 inches (50 cm) long.

To prevent fondant from becoming sticky, dust your work surface with confectioners' (icing) sugar before working with it.

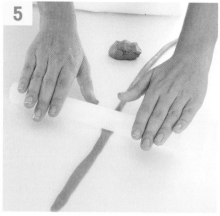

5

Using the rolling pin, gently roll along the top of each tube to flatten it, making a thin strip long enough to wrap around the cake.

6

Using water as glue, wrap the strips around the cake, placing one about one-third of the way up the cake and the other about two-thirds of the way up the cake.

7

Using the paintbrush, paint the strips with silver paint (being careful not to get paint on the brown fondant) and let dry for 25 to 30 minutes.

8

Fill the pastry bag with green icing and pipe grass around the base of the cake, reserving some green icing for step 16.

9

Place the chocolate cookies in a sealable plastic bag and use the rolling pin to crush them into crumbs. Spoon crumbs over the top of the cake to resemble soil.

10

Working from the top down, mold most of the blue fondant around the portion of the balloon stick that will not be covered by the watering can. Bend the stick to a natural pouring angle.

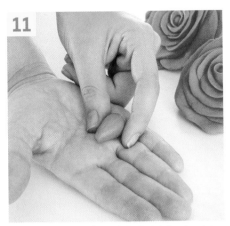

11

For each rose, roll ½ oz (15 g) pink fondant into a ball, then press the sides to form a teardrop shape.

12

Place another piece of fondant, slightly larger than the first, in your palm and use your thumb to flatten and form it into a thin petal shape.

13

Brush a teardrop with water and gently wrap the petal around it.

14

Repeat steps 12 and 13, using gradually larger pieces of fondant and placing the center of each new petal over the crease of the previous one, until you have used 5 oz (150 g) of fondant for each of 3 roses.

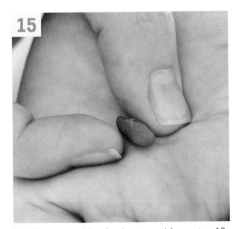

15

Use the excess blue fondant saved from step 10 to roll tiny water droplets between your finger and thumb.

16

Nestle the roses into the crumbs on the cake. Using water as glue, attach droplets to the cake and roses. Pipe a few sprouts of grass around the roses. Slide the spout of the watering can down the stick.

TIP

If you want to add a second layer of icing to the cake before applying the fondant, you will need an additional 1¼ cups (300 mL) icing for this recipe.

KNITTING BASKET

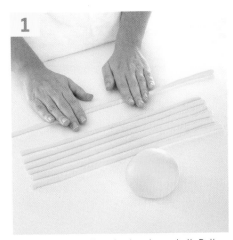

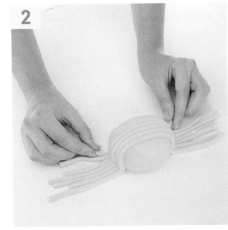

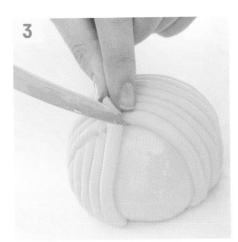

GETTING STARTED

Melt the candy wafers, attach the balloon stick to the center of the cake board and let set. Spread a small dollop of icing around the base of the stick. Center the first cake over the stick and slide it down the stick. Cover the top with icing. Center and slide the second cake down the stick. Crumb-coat the entire cake. Slide the 18-gauge wires down inside the stick and trim the stick and wires to the same height.

1 Roll half of the yellow fondant into a ball. Roll the other half into long, thin strings.

2 Using the pastry brush, brush the ball with water and wrap 6 to 8 strings over the ball, from left to right, leaving the front, back and bottom uncovered. Trim off excess string.

3 Attach strings vertically to the front and back of the ball, trimming them where they meet the strings on top. Cover each seam with 2 long strings and trim off excess. Set the excess fondant aside.

4 Repeat steps 1 to 3 with the purple and pink fondant. Set the yarn balls aside.

If you need to pay your grandma back for all those knitted sweaters you've collected over the years, this is the cake for you. Wow her with this awesome, colorful ode to her creative talents! Feeds 20.

EQUIPMENT

- Balloon stick
- 12-inch (30 cm) round cake board
- Three 18-gauge wires
- Pastry brush
- Rolling pin
- Cake smoother
- Basket weave–textured rolling pin
- 24 inches (60 cm) ribbon
- 2 plastic knitting needles
- Button fondant mold

INGREDIENTS

- 1 tbsp (15 mL) candy coating wafers
- 2 cups (500 mL) butter icing
- Two 8-inch (20 cm) round cakes, leveled
- 15 oz (450 g) yellow fondant
- Small bowl of water
- 15 oz (450 g) purple fondant
- 15 oz (450 g) pink fondant
- 35 oz (1 kg) brown fondant
- 2 oz (60 g) white fondant

TIPS

If desired, after step 6 cover the cake board with 10 oz (300 g) white fondant (see page 33).

If you want to add a second layer of icing to the cake before applying the fondant, you will need an additional 1¼ cups (300 mL) icing for this recipe.

To prevent fondant from becoming sticky, dust your work surface with confectioners' (icing) sugar before working with it.

If desired, after step 6 cover the cake board with 10 oz (300 g) white fondant (see page 33).

5

Using the regular rolling pin, roll out 24 oz (700 g) brown fondant into a sheet large enough to cover the entire cake.

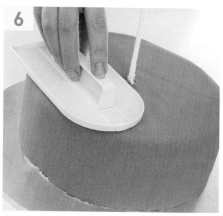

6

Slide the sheet down the balloon stick so it drapes over the cake. Use the cake smoother to smooth the top and sides of the cake. Trim off any excess fondant, setting it aside.

7

Roll the remaining brown fondant into a wide strip about 25 inches (63 cm) long. Measure the height of the cake and cut the strip to that width. Roll over the strip with the textured rolling pin.

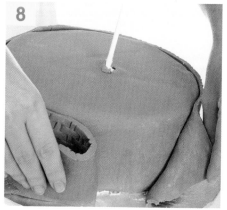

8

Brush the sides of the cake with water and gently wrap the strip around the cake, trimming off any excess.

9

Roll the excess brown fondant into 2 thick tubes about 28 inches (70 cm) long. Pinch one end of each tube together and twist the tubes around each other to create a cord. Pinch the open ends together.

10

Using water as glue, gently attach the cord to the top of the cake, around the perimeter. Trim off any excess fondant and press the ends of the cord together.

11

Starting from the top and working down, mold the white fondant around the balloon stick. Bend the stick slightly.

12

Cut the ribbon in half. Use one piece to tie the knitting needles together near the pointed ends (see tip). Use the other piece to tie the needles to the top of the balloon stick. Cut off excess ribbon.

13

Using water as glue, place the yarn balls on the cake around the balloon stick.

14

Using the button mold, create several buttons from small pieces of excess yellow, purple and pink fondant. Using water as glue, attach them to the cake and cake board as desired.

15

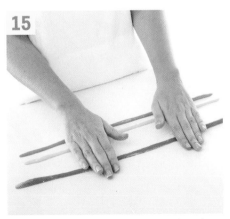

Roll the remaining excess yellow, purple and pink fondant into long, thin strings.

16

Brush the white fondant on the stick with water and attach the strings to the stick (see tip).

TIPS

In step 12, intertwine the ribbon between the knitting needles, wrapping it around them and tying multiple knots to make sure it holds firm.

In step 16, use the strings to hide the ribbon at the top of the stick and around the needles, and let them hang all the way down the stick to the surface of the cake, covering the white fondant completely. You will need to keep dampening the strings as you attach them.

If you would like to hide the seam on the side of the cake, simply attach some extra fondant strings to trail from the top of the cake over the side, hiding the seam.

CHIC HANDBAG

GETTING STARTED

Melt 1 tbsp (15 mL) candy wafers, attach the balloon stick to the center of the cake board and let set. Spread a small dollop of icing around the base of the stick. Cover the top of the cake with icing and cut the cake in half vertically. Place the halves on either side of the balloon stick so the iced sides are facing each other and the flat ends are down. Crumb-coat the entire cake. Slide the 18-gauge wires down inside the stick and trim the stick and wires to the height of the coin purse plus about 5 inches (12.5 cm) from the top of the cake.

Here's the ideal gravity cake for anyone who loves to shop! Practice your fondant techniques and design a dream purse for your favorite shopaholic. Feeds 12.

EQUIPMENT

- Balloon stick
- 12-inch (30 cm) round cake board
- Three 18-gauge wires
- Small display coin purse
- Rolling pin
- Cake smoother
- Small paintbrush
- Gold edible paint

INGREDIENTS

- 3 tbsp (45 mL) candy coating wafers
- 1¼ cups (300 mL) butter icing
- 8-inch (20 cm) round cake, leveled
- Confectioners' (icing) sugar
- 18 oz (525 g) white fondant
- 8 oz (250 g) black fondant
- Small bowl of water
- Eleven to twelve ½-oz (15 g) foil-wrapped chocolate coins

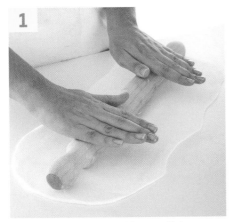

Dust your work surface with sugar. Using the rolling pin, roll out 13 oz (400 g) white fondant into a sheet large enough to cover the entire cake.

Slide the sheet down the balloon stick so it drapes over the cake. Use the cake smoother to smooth the top and sides of the cake. Trim off any excess fondant. Smooth again.

Roll out the black fondant until thin and smooth. Cut two 1-inch (2.5 cm) wide strips as long as the front base of the cake and two more as long as the base at the sides.

Using water as glue, attach the strips across the base of the cake, trimming off any excess length. Use your fingers to blend the seams together.

TIPS

If you want to add a second layer of icing to the cake before applying the fondant, you will need an additional ⅔ cup (150 mL) icing for this recipe.

When cutting strips in steps 3, 5, 6 and 14, use a clean plastic ruler to help you cut straight lines.

As you are working with the black fondant, reroll the scraps as necessary before cutting more strips.

5

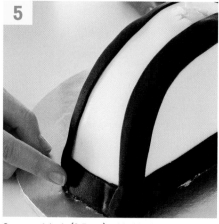

Cut two 1-inch (2.5 cm) wide black strips as long as the top arc of the cake. Attach them to the top of the cake, draping along the edges of the arc to meet the strips at the base. Blend the seams.

6

Cut two ½-inch (1 cm) wide black strips, about 4½ inches (11 cm) long. Stand the strips on edge at the top of the cake, running them lengthwise in an arc around the stick. Pinch the ends together.

7

Cut a 1-inch (2.5 cm) wide, 2-inch (5 cm) long black strip. Cut off 2 of the corners on a diagonal, so the strip looks like the end of a belt.

8

Using a fork, stamp holes around the sides and narrow end of the strip.

9

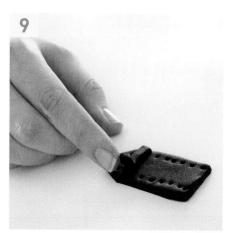

Cut a thin strip of fondant slightly longer than the width of the belt. Using water as glue, attach the strip near the bottom of the belt.

10

Using water as glue, attach the belt to the front of the cake, with the top edge of the belt aligned with the top of the arc.

11 Using your hands, roll 1 oz (30 g) white fondant into a 10-inch (25 cm) long tube. Cut the tube into five 2-inch (5 cm) pieces. Roll one piece slightly thinner. Bend each piece into a wide U shape.

12 Using water as glue, attach the thinner U to the belt, with the ends touching the strap.

TIPS

If your fondant starts to get sticky, keep dusting your work surface with confectioners' (icing) sugar.

To clean any confectioners' (icing) sugar or marks off the black fondant, wipe it gently with water.

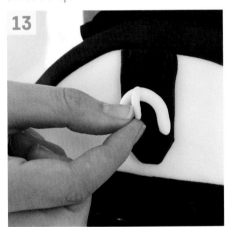

13 Form an extra pinch of white fondant into a thin tube and attach it vertically in the center of the belt, between the U and the strap.

14 Cut two 1-inch (2.5 cm) wide, 9-inch (23 cm) long black strips. Dampen the fondant on the front and back of the cake. Attach each strip like a purse strap, with the ends rising about ½ inch (1 cm) above the black border.

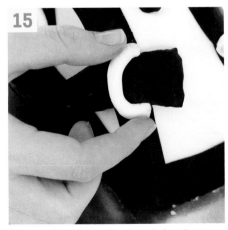

15 Place a white U around each end of each strap, using water as glue to attach the U to the top border of the cake.

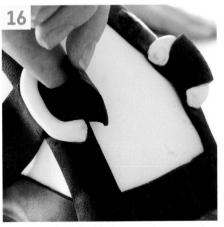

16 Fold the ends of the black straps down over the white Us, and use water to seal them down.

TIPS

If desired, after step 17 cover the cake board with 13 oz (400 g) light pink fondant (see page 33). You may also wish to press it with a fondant impression mat in a pretty texture.

When attaching the coins to the balloon stick in step 21, take your time and give each piece time to set before adding another piece above it. If the melted candy starts to harden, add a drop of vegetable oil and reheat.

Using the paintbrush, paint the white buckle pieces and white strap holders with gold paint.

Using the rolling pin, roll out the remaining white fondant until smooth and very thin. Cut several 2-inch (5 cm) squares and gently crimp the sides together, to resemble crumpled tissue paper.

Melt the remaining candy wafers. Using the melted candy as glue, attach the foil-wrapped chocolate coins to the fondant on the balloon stick.

Starting near the top and working down, mold 2 oz (60 oz) white fondant around the balloon stick.

Dampen the fondant around the balloon stick, inside the black strips, and gently attach the tissue paper pieces.

Slide the coin purse down the stick. If you have extra chocolate coins, attach them to the cake board.

GUMBALL MACHINE

GETTING STARTED

Spread some icing on the 12-inch (30 cm) cake board where the cake will sit, to prevent it from sliding. Stack the 4 cakes in the center of the board, smothering icing between each layer. Using a serrated knife and starting about 1 inch (2.5 cm) from the edge at the top of the cake, carve downward at an angle to make the top of the cake narrower than the bottom, ensuring it is even all the way around. Crumb-coat the entire cake. Let stand for 1 hour or until thawed completely.

EQUIPMENT

- 12-inch (30 cm) round cake board
- Serrated knife
- Rolling pin
- Cake smoother
- Three 6-inch (15 cm) cake pop sticks
- Pastry brush
- 1-inch (2.5 cm) circle cutter
- 3-inch (7.5 cm) thin round cake board (or cut to size)
- 3-quart (3 L) transparent plastic bowl
- Balloon stick
- Three 18-gauge wires
- Small lightweight paper bag

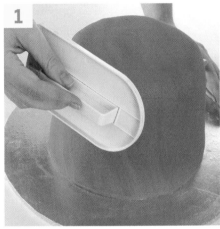

1 Using the rolling pin, roll out 35 oz (1 kg) red fondant into a sheet large enough to cover the entire cake. Drape the sheet over the cake, smooth the fondant and trim off any excess. Smooth again.

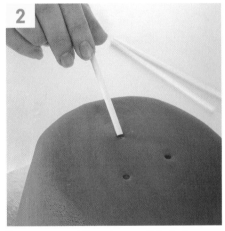

2 If necessary, cut the cake pop sticks to the exact height of the cake. Make small indents in a triangle on top of the cake, making sure the triangle is centered and no larger than the 3-inch (7.5 cm) cake board.

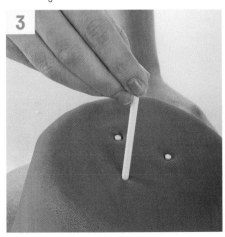

3 Slide the cake pop sticks into the marked indents on the cake, pushing them all the way down to the cake board.

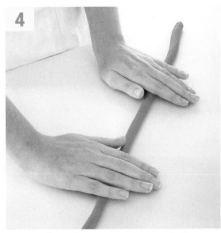

4 Roll 4 oz (125 g) red fondant into a tube long enough to wrap around the base of the cake (about 22 inches/55 cm long).

INGREDIENTS

- 2 cups (500 mL) butter icing
- Four 7-inch (18 cm) round cakes, leveled and frozen
- 45 oz (1.3 kg) red fondant
- Small bowl of water
- 2 oz (60 g) gray fondant

continued on next page

INGREDIENTS

- ½ oz (15 g) black fondant
- 3½ lbs (1.75 kg) gumballs
- 3 tbsp (45 mL) royal icing mix
- 4 oz (125 g) white fondant
- 2 tbsp (30 mL) candy coating wafers

TIPS

If you want to add a second layer of icing to the cake before applying the fondant, you will need an additional 2½ cups (625 mL) icing for this recipe.

To prevent fondant from becoming sticky, dust your work surface with confectioners' (icing) sugar before working with it.

If desired, after step 5 cover the cake board with 10 oz (300 g) white fondant (see page 33).

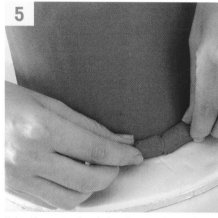

5

Using the pastry brush, brush water in a strip around the base of the cake. Wrap the tube tightly around the base. Trim off any excess fondant and press the ends of the tube together.

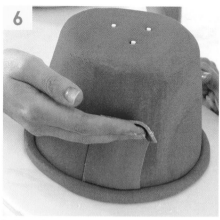

6

Roll out the gray fondant, then cut out a rectangle with long sides ½ inch (1 cm) shorter than the cake. Using water as glue, attach the rectangle vertically to the front of the cake, above the tube.

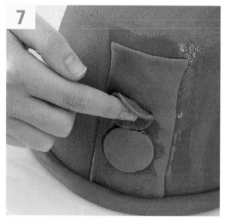

7

Reroll the excess gray fondant and, using the circle cutter, cut out 2 circles. Attach the circles, one above the other, centrally on the gray rectangle.

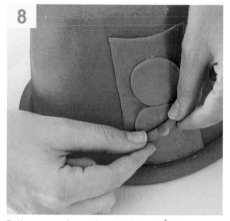

8

Roll a scrap of gray fondant into a 1½-inch (4 cm) long tube. Form another scrap into a tiny circle. Attach the circle to the center of the tube. Attach the tube horizontally in the center of the lower gray circle.

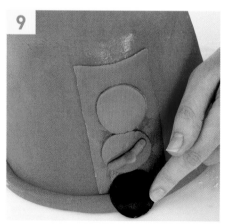

9

Roll out the black fondant and, using the circle cutter, cut out a circle. Using water as glue, attach the black circle directly below the lower gray circle.

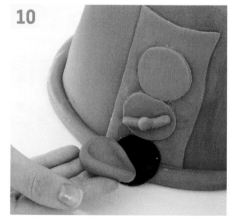

10

Form ½ oz (15 g) red fondant into a shallow bowl. Flatten one side of the bowl. Attach the bowl to the cake board with the flat side against the black circle. Place a gumball in the bowl.

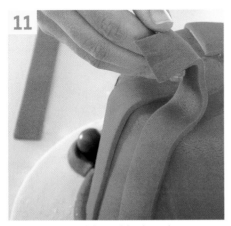

11

Roll out the remaining red fondant, then cut it into nine 1-inch (2.5 cm) wide strips. Using water as glue, attach the strips vertically to the sides of the cake and into the center (see tip). Let set for 1 hour.

12

Combine royal icing mix and 2 tsp (10 mL) water. Spoon a dollop in the center of the cake and center the 3-inch (7.5 cm) cake board on top. Spoon another dollop on the board and set the plastic bowl on top.

13

Mold 2 oz (60 g) white fondant around the balloon stick's base. Dampen the bottom of the bowl and press the fondant down lightly over the damp spot (see tip). Fill the bowl half full with gumballs.

14

Slide the wires inside the stick and trim the stick and wires to the height of the paper bag plus about 7 inches (18 cm) from the top of the gumballs.

15

Working from the top down, mold the remaining white fondant around the portion of the stick that will not be covered by the paper bag.

16

Melt the candy wafers. Using the candy as glue, attach the remaining gumballs to the fondant on the stick (see tip). Slide the paper bag down the stick.

TIPS

In step 11, attach the first 2 strips on either side of the gray rectangle, exactly the same distance from it. Attach the strips vertically from the top of the tube at the base of the cake up the side of the cake and into the center. Attach the remaining 7 strips an equal distance apart, working your way around each side to the back of the cake. Trim off any overlap at the top.

In step 13, you want to make sure the stick is firmly attached to the bottom of the bowl, but be careful not to push too hard and squash your cake!

When attaching the gumballs to the balloon stick in step 16, take your time and give each piece time to set before adding another piece above it. If the melted candy starts to harden, add a drop of vegetable oil and reheat.

Acknowledgments

We would like to send a huge, heartfelt thank you to all of the wonderful people who have come together to create this book, especially the entire Robert Rose team — Bob Dees, Marian Jarkovich, Nina McCreath and Martine Quibell — as well as editor Sue Sumeraj, recipe editor Jennifer MacKenzie, photographer Neil Langan and designer Kevin Cockburn of PageWave Graphics.

Thank you to Marilyn Allen for believing in us. Without you, this book wouldn't have been possible.

Thank you to our wonderful families, partners and friends, and everyone who has helped us with everything from limitless messy kitchens to babysitting duties. Your love and support throughout this journey kept us going, and we dedicate this book to all of you!

Library and Archives Canada Cataloguing in Publication

Friedman, Jakki, 1985-, author
   Gravity cakes! : create 45 amazing cakes / Jakki Friedman & Francesca Librae.

Includes index.
ISBN 978-0-7788-0549-6 (paperback)

   1. Cake. 2. Cookbooks.
I. Librae, Francesca, 1986-, author II. Title. III. Title: Create forty-five amazing cakes.

TX771.F75 2017   641.86'53   C2016-906392-5

Index

HAPPY
DECORATING!